ADVANCE PRAISE

"If you have students who have grown apathetic toward writing because they see writing as only a means to a grade or test score, you need to read *Creating Confident Writers*. Drawing on years of classroom practice and best practice research, *Creating Confident Writers* will help restore your students' (and your own!) confidence in writing again by showing you what really matters in writing—the writer."

**—Jennifer Laffin, Founder of Teach Write LLC
and Co-Moderator of the #TeachWrite Twitter Chat**

"Far too many students walk into our classes in September sure that they are 'not writers.' Before the year has begun, they have admitted defeat, and in doing so, they will inevitably slow their growth as writers. Getting these students to believe that they are indeed writers too has long been one of the most daunting challenges for writing teachers—until now. In this book that you hold, Troy Hicks and Andy Schoenborn have created something rare and remarkable: a practical, deeply-researched handbook for how to turn all of our writers into more confident and competent ones."

**—Matthew Johnson, author of *Flash Feedback:
Responding to Student Writing Better and Faster–Without Burning Out***

"Hicks and Schoenborn know that high-quality writing instruction isn't 'done' to students; rather, it is a supportive process of invitation, encouragement, and celebration. As teachers, we intuitively understand the link between confidence and success, but to what extent do we design our classrooms, lessons, and feedback to prioritize writers' confidence over everything else? We're thankful for a book that undertakes this more-important-than-ever work of building writers' courage. From sample class schedules to direct-to-class writing invitations to language for building confident writers in inclusive classrooms, *Creating Confident Writers* provides plentiful, practical tools to invite, encourage, and celebrate our writers to be their most confident selves."

**—Allison Marchetti and Rebekah O'Dell, founders of Moving Writers,
authors of *Writing with Mentors* and *Beyond Literary Analysis***

"Guided by their own experiences, and especially their great humility, Troy Hicks and Andy Schoenborn demonstrate their reverence for the written word and more importantly, their deep regard for the learners they serve in *Creating Confident Writers*. Offering new insights on purpose and form, the use of print and digital technologies, and the way we create communities of writers, this book is inspiration and practical application in equal measure."

**—Angela Stockman, MSEd, former middle and high school teacher, founder of
the WNY Young Writers Studio, professional learning facilitator, and author**

"As I read *Creating Confident Writers: For High School, College, and Life* by Troy Hicks and Andy Schoenborn I realized that I was engaged in an active conversation with these two brilliant teacher/authors; I nodded and whispered 'yes' a half dozen times, dog-eared most of the pages, scribbled copious notes in the margins, and found myself energized to inspire, encourage, and celebrate all student writers. Perhaps adding an additional subtitle would be appropriate: *Creating Confident Teachers of Writing*."

—Georgia Heard, MFA Writing, Columbia University, author of
Awakening the Heart: Exploring Poetry in Elementary and Middle School
and *Heart Maps: Helping Students Create and Craft Authentic Writing*

"Weaving wise beliefs with ideas-to-try now, *Creating Confident Writers* by Andy Schoenborn and Troy Hicks perfectly balances inspiration with application. Each page brims with possibility and promise, respect and reality, clearing teaching trails that invite, encourage, and celebrate all voices. In a time when our young people struggle to find meaning, this book offers hope along with specific keys that can help us all find and make significance through the very human act of writing."

—Amy Ludwig VanDerwater, author of *Poems Are Teachers:*
How Studying Poetry Strengthens Writing in All Genres

"For secondary and college teachers who wonder if the Writing Workshop provides viable instruction, even for AP English, this book proclaims (with evidence): yes, it does. Teacher-writers Hicks and Schoenborn explain how to create conditions that all writers need: support for making decisions; authentic, encouraging feedback; and opportunities to publish to the world. This book overflows with student writing, dozens of links to resources, and joyful demonstrations of teaching writing processes and products that feel engaging and significant."

—Katherine Bomer, Literacy Consultant, author of
The Journey is Everything: Teaching Essays that Students Want to
Write for People Who Want to Read Them* and *Writing a Life: Teaching Memoir

"Troy Hicks and Andy Schoenborn have written a book about about writing—and teaching writing—that finally shows us what it looks like to design writing assignments that engage and educate students, that integrate technology and teaching without reducing either to mere activities. This book will create not only more confident writers but teachers who will feel more confident as they design writing assignments and teach writing."

—Jim Burke, author of *The English Teacher's Companion*
and *The Six Academic Writing Assignments: Designing the User's Journey*

CREATING CONFIDENT WRITERS

NORTON BOOKS IN EDUCATION

CREATING CONFIDENT WRITERS

For High School, College, and Life

Troy Hicks and Andy Schoenborn

W. W. NORTON & COMPANY
Independent Publishers Since 1923

For information about permission to reproduce selections from this book, write to
Permissions, W. W. Norton & Company, Inc., 500 Fifth Avenue, New York, NY 10110

For information about special discounts for bulk purchases, please contact
W. W. Norton Special Sales at specialsales@wwnorton.com or 800-233-4830

Manufacturing by Sheridan Books
Book design by Joe Lops
Production manager: Katelyn MacKenzie

Library of Congress Cataloging-in-Publication Data

Names: Hicks, Troy, author. | Schoenborn, Andy author.
Title: Creating confident writers for high school, college, and life /
Troy Hicks and Andy Schoenborn. Description: First edition. |
New York : W.W. Norton & Company, 2020. | Series: Norton books in
education | Includes bibliographical references and index.
Identifiers: LCCN 2019030056 | ISBN 9780393714166 (paperback) |
ISBN 9780393714173 (epub)
Subjects: LCSH: Composition (Language arts)—Study and teaching (Secondary) |
English language—Composition and exercises—Study and teaching (Secondary) |
Composition (Language arts)—Study and teaching (Higher) |
English language—Composition and exercises—Study and teaching (Higher)
Classification: LCC LB1631 .H493 2020 | DDC 428.0071/2—dc23
LC record available at https://lccn.loc.gov/2019030056

W. W. Norton & Company, Inc., 500 Fifth Avenue, New York, N.Y. 10110
www.wwnorton.com

W. W. Norton & Company Ltd., 15 Carlisle Street, London W1D 3BS

1 2 3 4 5 6 7 8 9 0

For my sons who are in their final years of high school— Beau, Shane, and Cooper—and who may not always share my same passion for reading and writing. ;-)

Please know how much I enjoy it when you ask me to look over the occasional essay or share the idea that maybe, just maybe, you feel the book you are reading in English class isn't so bad after all.

—T. H.

For my students, past and present, whom I continue to learn with. For my children, Dean, Kendal, Olivia, and Everly, who encourage me. And, to my wife, Julie, whose unwavering love and support made this book possible.

—A. S.

Contents

SECTION 3: CELEBRATE

Foreword

Everything I need to know about writing I learned in Mrs. Goldman's third-grade class, Greenbriar School, Northbrook, IL, 1979.

Mrs. Goldman gave us a task, to write instructions for a peanut butter and jelly sandwich, and then she produced the sandwich fixings and told us to go ahead and make our sandwiches... *following our directions to the letter.*

Most, maybe even all of us, had left some things out. Things like what you are supposed to spread the peanut butter on the bread with, or how much peanut butter and jelly to use, or which sides of the peanut butter and jelly covered bread should be pressed together.

I have a picture of me in the midst of the experience, wearing a red-checked plaid flannel, a messy mop of blond hair covering my ears. Because I am smiling you can see my wayward front teeth, traumatized in a skateboard accident so badly that I would get braces for the first of two times the next year.

My hand is knuckles deep inside a jar of peanut butter because I am one of the people who forgot to say that one should use a knife to spread the peanut butter across the bread. I am smiling as a classmate looks on at my foolishness.

In that moment, something clicked about writing. I understood that there is a purpose behind what we write; that our writing must be useful to others. I understood that in order to be useful to others we must consider our audience prior, during, and after the act of writing. I learned these things in a flash of discovery and they have been with me ever since.

They have served me well. They kicked off a writing journey that shows no signs of stopping.

Some things have changed in the intervening forty years. My hair is nearly gray now, and I keep it above my ears. With the prevalence of peanut allergies, I cannot imagine a teacher encouraging her students to shove their hands in a jar of peanut butter.

Based on my twenty-five or so years working with first-year college students, I think something else has changed. Not many of the students I work with would have ever smiled while doing anything writing-related in school. They arrive in our first-year writing class having internalized writing for school as a grim slog through proficiencies, laden with prescriptions meant to help them pass assessments, assessments that seem far removed from the kind of liberation of discovery I routinely experienced during my school years.

They are not confident writers; even the ones who report getting good grades do not have a self-concept of being a writer at all. They are instead "students," performing to meet the standards, jumping through one hoop and the next. What they describe is depersonalized, joyless, and sort of heartbreaking as I think about how, for me, writing has consistently been a source of personal liberation since third grade.

Even when I was writing for the purpose of assessment, I knew that I was capable of more. Sure, I can jump through that hoop, but watch me set it on fire as I cruise by.

The underlying causes of my students' attitudes toward writing are myriad, systemic, and could fill a book. I know this because I wrote one, and upon its appearance in the world I began to hear from teachers expressing nearly identical frustrations, teachers who were looking for a way out from under these systemic pressures that seem to separate student writing from the joyous and genuinely rigorous activity it can and should be.

We must collectively do better by our teachers to remove the constraints and provide the necessary resources so teachers can work with their students as the professionals they are.

I believe this will happen—because it must happen—but in the meantime, we need to do our best under conditions as they are, which is why I'm so pleased to see *Creating Confident Writers* enter into the world.

Invite. Encourage. Celebrate. These are the three principles of *Creating Confident Writers*, and I know they work because this is what Mrs. Goldman did for me and my classmates forty years ago. She trusted us with the work of writing and therefore we became writers.

In *Creating Confident Writers*, I see a book that is both concise and filled with concrete and actionable approaches that will help classrooms embody the values of *invite, encourage, celebrate.* It provides ways for us to treat students not as students, but as fully-fledged humans. It respects teacher autonomy and class difference and provides a framework for thinking about writing that can be adapted to any classroom and occasion.

Now, we should not think any of this will be easy. I did not leave Mrs. Goldman's classroom as a fully-formed writer. Neither will adopting this book be a sufficient step by itself. It is the start of a journey for everyone involved. *Creating Confident Writers* is an invitation that puts students and their learning central to the process.

Forty years past my epiphany in Mrs. Goldman's class, I do not think I am a fully-formed writer. I am continually frustrated by my inability to achieve that which I intend with words, but I've never wavered in my belief in the process. Similarly, as a teacher, I learn something new about how to better engage students every semester. It is sometimes difficult to know that there is no terminal proficiency, but it is also energizing to know there's always more to be learned.

The simultaneous difficulty of writing and the joy in using writing to connect to others, even it's merely how to make a peanut butter and jelly sandwich, is worth celebrating on a daily basis.

I am grateful to Troy Hicks and Andy Schoenborn for providing a book that helps us plan, experience, and achieve these feats worthy of celebration.

—John Warner
Author of *Why They Can't Write:*
Killing the Five-Paragraph Essay and Other Necessities

Preface

Through countless collegial conversations, conference sessions and work-shops, Twitter chats and webinars, and—most importantly—hours spent with our own students, the two of us have learned how to teach writing. What we will demonstrate in this book is that, in order to create confident writers, we as educators must embody three stances:

- A stance of invitation, in which we welcome writers into genuine inquiry around texts and topics of their choosing;
- A stance of encouragement, in which we strengthen writers through sustained feedback aimed at improvement;
- A stance of celebration, in which we honor writers when they take risks, try new writing techniques, and make their work public.

Why, in our effort to create confident writers, do we take these stances as teachers of writing? There is far more history than we can cover in this preface, as we want to welcome you, our colleagues who teach writing to high school and college students, into dialogue about this work. Thus, we answer the "why" question in a necessarily succinct manner, and limit our direct response to this preface (though we hope you will see the answer to the "why" question threaded throughout the rest of our book!).

To begin addressing what it means to create confident writers, we need to think about the conditions that occur in our classrooms and schools that inhibit them. For instance, in the title of his 2018 book, journalist and college composition instructor John Warner reframes the age-old question about our students and their abilities. *Why They Can't Write* opens with the conclusion that "[t]here seems to be widespread agreement that when it comes to the writing skills of college students, and even recent college graduates, we are in the midst of a crisis" (2018, p. 1).

Research studies, stories from the news media, standardized test scores, and evidence from students, teachers, parents, policy makers, and employers have shown this for decades. We've been asking "why" for what seems like forever: why "Johnny can't write" (to hearken back to the famous *Newsweek* exposé [Sheils, 1975]), why we have a nation at risk (National Commission on Excellence in Education, 1983), why children are being left behind (United States Department of Education, 2002), why there is a "neglected 'R'" in our schools (National Commission on Writing for America's Families, Schools, and Colleges, 2003), or why we are still bound up in a culture of standardized testing.

To put this in the context of research in English education, we have numerous studies that point to what works in high-quality writing instruction and what doesn't, drawing from large-scale research studies (e.g., Applebee, 1981; Applebee & Langer, 2011; Graham et al., 2016; Graham & Perin, 2007; Hillocks, 1986) and the wisdom of teacher-researchers, many of whom we will return to later in the book (e.g., Atwell, 1998, 2014; J. Burke, 2003, 2012; Gallagher, 2006, 2011; Gallagher & Kittle, 2018; Kittle, 2008; Marchetti & O'Dell, 2015). There are, no doubt, countless pressures—both historical and contemporary, from outside our schools as well as inside our own classrooms—that tell us the task of teaching writing and, in turn, creating confident writers is nearly impossible. There are many ways in which we could dwell on the skills our students lack, the unfortunate ways in which they've experienced writing instruction in the past, or their general malaise when it comes to creativity, risk-taking, and inquiry.

However, we are taking a different approach. Indeed, we begin this book offering our stances in a posture of grace and humility, noting that the lessons we share, the student voices we highlight, and the questions we pose are ones that drive us in our teaching, at both the high school and the college level, and that different classrooms, communities, and contexts may—indeed, will—need to extend and adapt our approaches. Our goal in *Creating Confident Writers* is to look forward, to consider the ways in which we—Andy, as a high school teacher of students ranging from freshman English to AP Literature, and Troy, as a college professor teaching everyone from freshman writers to graduate students—can share some of our practices and principles with you.

We have been fortunate enough to spend time together observing each other's teaching, facilitating professional development workshops, and collaborating as coauthors. Through these experiences, we hope to share some stories from our classrooms, bringing the voices of our students into the conversation, and opening that dialogue to you, our readers, as well. And we want to illustrate and continually reiterate the three main actions that we take when working with our student writers: we invite, we encourage, and we celebrate. Day in and day out, these stances guide our work.

As teachers of writing, we know that creating confident writers begins well before our students walk in the door on the first day of school. The ways in which we plan the overarching goals for our course, the daily routines, the specific assignments, the opportunities for interaction, and the celebrations, both small and large, will all contribute to an overall feeling, a classroom community that encourages writers to support one another and to strive for more. Throughout, you will find examples of how we each choose to do this in our own classrooms, exploring samples of student work that have been produced, and hearing more about how we strive to enact the principles we learned through our work with professional organizations like the National Writing Project and the National Council of Teachers of English, and guiding policy documents such as *The Framework for Success in Postsecondary Writing* (Council of Writing Program Administrators, National Council of Teachers of English, & National Writing Project, 2011), which we will refer to as the *Framework*, and the *Professional Knowledge for the Teaching of Writing* (National Council of Teachers of English, 2016b) which we will refer to as *Professional Knowledge*. We are grateful to the leaders of these professional organizations for allowing us to cite these documents extensively in our book.

In building from these perspectives, we aim to show how we create confident writers in our classrooms and how we share common ground. Much has been said over the years about the divide between the expectations of writing in high school and in college. Of course, there are some differences. Yet, on the whole, we find that a consistent, steady approach to high-quality writing instruction in all classrooms, from elementary and middle school into high school and beyond, is what yields the greatest results. These three principles, these actions—inviting, encouraging, celebrating—form the foundation of our writing instruction.

Throughout the book, we will show these principles coming alive in our classrooms, connect you to other teachers and researchers who embody these ideas, and offer insights on how you can adopt these stances in your own teaching, all in the service of creating confident writers.

We thank a number of people here who have invited us to share and supported us along the way:

- Carol Chambers Collins, Editor at Norton Books in Education. Having first met Carol in 2014, Troy is grateful for her patience, flexibility, and continued support in efforts to bring this book to print. Great ideas take time as well as kind, encouraging editors.

- Members of the Norton team, especially Sara McBride, who helped coordinate permissions, and Nancy Palmquist, who served as our copy editor. We appreciate your attention to detail, bringing clarity and concision to our work. We also thank Mariah Eppes and Jamie Vincent, as well as all the other colleagues at Norton who have helped bring this book to press.

- Colleagues in our local and national professional networks who have inspired our ideas and asked us about our writing process. There are too many of you to name, and we don't want to overlook anyone, so we share a hearty "thank you" with everyone including our local colleagues from the Chippewa River Writing Project at Central Michigan University and the Michigan Council of Teachers of English, as well as our extended professional network through the National Council of Teachers of English, the National Writing Project, and numerous online communities, including Teach Write.

- We thank colleagues at the National Council of Teachers of English, the National Writing Project, and the Council of Writing Program Administrators who granted us permission to freely and extensively draw quotes from *The Framework for Success in Postsecondary Writing* as well as *Professional Knowledge for the Teaching of Writing*.

- Thanks to Dr. Stephanie West-Puckett of the University of Rhode Island for allowing us to quote extensively from her assignments, originally released under a Creative Commons license, which Troy relied on while developing his own writing intensive course.

- To all the students who shared their work, we appreciate your willingness to take risks as writers and to share your ideas in our book. We have permission to identify all of you by name, in the text itself, and we are grateful that—even though we could provide you with no other compensation—you are able to be acknowledged in this way.

- And, as most writers do, we thank our families for allowing us the time, space, and opportunity for writing. Our hope is that, for our own children, the ideas we share in this book may reach the classrooms in which you read, write, and learn.

Introduction

We are coming to understand more and more that our students, both high school and college, come to our classrooms with their own life experiences and literacy practices, some of which will be similar to their classmates' and some of which will be very different. Culturally sustaining pedagogies (Paris & Alim, 2017), trauma-informed teaching (Goodman & Fine, 2018), growth mindsets (Dweck, 2007), and a number of other foci in research literature and popular conversations about education remind us that, in order to create confident writers, we need to consider a variety of factors in the contemporary classroom.

Given this evolving understanding of our students, classrooms, and communities, we acknowledge that teaching writing is hard work, and it has been hard work forever. What we need to consider today is no different than what teachers of writing have had to keep in mind for over a century. We are reminded of the opening page of the first issue of the *English Journal*, in 1912, in which Edwin Hopkins asked: "Can Good Composition Teaching Be Done under Present Conditions?" His answer then? A simple "no" (Hopkins, 1912). He elaborates on the numerous reasons it is difficult, in particular that "under present conditions, composition teachers have from two and a half to three times as many people as they should" (4). Sadly, given the "present conditions" over one hundred years later, we concur.

Thus, over the decades, teaching writing has not become any easier. In his book *Why They Can't Write: Killing the Five-Paragraph Essay and Other Necessities*, journalist and writing teacher John Warner offers a succinct, if blunt assessment of what it means to be a teacher of writing:

Teaching, like writing, is an extended exercise in failure. You make a plan, do your best to execute, have some portion of your ass handed to you by circumstances and events you could not foresee, and try to do better next time around. (122)

From there, he documents extensive examples, continuing to show how the teaching of writing is complicated work. From whole-class lessons to individual or small-group conferences, to feedback and assessment, the decisions continue to multiply each day, and discouragement can set in quickly. Both of us, Andy and Troy, with a combined total of over thirty years in middle, high school, and college writing classrooms, still feel the sensation of having parts of ourselves—including the part that Warner eloquently notes, as well as our hearts and souls—handed to us each day. We do not have all the answers, but we keep asking questions and looking for possibilities.

Creating Confident Writers is our attempt to distill some of what works for our students, within our teaching contexts. Noting that all classrooms, schools, and communities have unique variations, we hope our ideas are both practical and flexible. We offer these strategies and pose challenging questions as a way for us to share what we have learned from our own classroom inquiry and from substantive professional learning through organizations such as the National Writing Project, the National Council of Teachers of English, the Council of Writing Program Administrators, and the research literature.

Later in this introduction we will frame our thinking for the entire book by exploring two foundational documents: *The Framework for Success in Postsecondary Writing* and *Professional Knowledge for the Teaching of Writing*. We will then explain our three stances that help create confidence in our writers—invite, encourage, celebrate—and, finally, we will offer a preview of the remaining chapters. Before all of this, we do take Warner's point that teaching can feel like an "extended exercise in failure" and that the contemporary writing classroom is a complex place. Yet we don't dwell there for long. By recognizing our current context, we can make meaningful progress toward change. Moving the writers in our classrooms, as well as ourselves, toward confidence: these are the dual foci of *Creating Confident Writers*.

In our work together, we have come to believe that open and informed conversations about writing practices between high school teachers and college/university writing teachers is critical. In dialogue, we can create confident writers. We welcome continued conversation about the ideas shared here through the authors' website and via the #creatingconfidentwriters hashtag.

Considering the Contemporary Writing Classroom

We need to create safe, caring spaces for writers to share their words. We need to offer them choice and provide mentor texts. And we need to help them see that writing can be for an audience other than a teacher and for a purpose beyond simply getting a grade. That much has remained the same from the time of Hopkins, through generations of English teachers, up to Warner and thousands of others who, like us today, find ourselves in classrooms facing new challenges.

We know, both empirically and from experience, that the condition and health of students' socio-emotional lives are equally, if not more, important than the academic skills and the content or facts we can teach them. In addition to our broadened sense of perspective on issues related to culture, trauma, and psychology, we are two decades into the twenty-first century. The massive changes in literacy practice—as well as the technologies and high-speed access that would allow them to work—are, while not perfectly distributed, almost ubiquitous (Jiang, 2018). And, speaking of facts, we are now in a "post-truth" world, where political ideology has rooted itself in a new form of divisive discourse.

Moreover, kids are finding it more and more difficult to connect with school, at least as it is currently imagined and enacted. One anonymous high school student from a 2017 survey admitted, "The things we learn help us pass tests so we can get a good grade, but we don't learn basic skills for studying that will help us survive in college." The reality is that very few standardized tests are given beyond high school, and the on-demand writing expectations of those tests are rarely found beyond the SAT or ACT. Yet, far too often, ninth through eleventh grade high school teachers yield to the pressures to raise standardized testing scores. This leaves behind student passion, exploration, and agency in the wake of test data.

While our very brief summation of these trends could be seen as dismissive, our goal for this introduction is not to document all the sociological phenomena that affect our students, as that could go on for pages. Suffice it to say, there are many reasons that we need to reconsider what we do in our classrooms, with and for students, in order to create confident writers.

In this introduction, we set the foundation for the conversation that will follow through the book. Many of the examples will be drawn from Andy's high school classroom, as Troy has been observing and learning with Andy during visits over the years and especially in the fall of 2018. Some examples will be drawn from Troy's seminar for freshmen, taught at the university level. All are born of our combined thirty-plus years of experience as writers and teachers of writing. It is from these experiences that we have come to some considerations about what it takes to create confident writers through an ongoing process of inviting, encouraging, and celebrating them and their work. These are the stances that guide us as educators and that will become themes tying together all the activities and ideas we share here.

So, it is worth spending some time thinking about each of these actions, these stances, as we begin, and open up a dialogue with you, our colleagues and fellow teachers of writing.

Our Stances for Creating Confident Writers: Invite, Encourage, Celebrate

In the countless conversations, revisions, and hours that have led to the words in these pages, the two of us have discussed many lessons, assignments, and samples of student work. Here, we boil them down to three key themes that help create confident writers: invitation, encouragement, and celebration.

First, with the idea of *invitation*, we work from a stance that lets students know that they do not "have" to engage in a particular writing task, but that they are invited to do so. Yes, in some ways we realize that this is just a play on words, as we still hold the power of grades over our students whether they "choose" to engage with the tasks we lay out or not. However, we contend that framing writing tasks as genuine invitations, with opportunities for choice, in turn empowers writers to make choices. They are made to know that their presence is welcome and that we look forward to hearing their voices in our classrooms.

Second, we *encourage*. If anything about being writers and teachers of writing resonates for the two of us, it is that the inner critic is always present, and that sharing our work with an audience is the only way to know, one way or the other, whether that critic is right. As the entire genre and industry of self-help books shows, we all need encouragement in some way, shape, or form. High school and college students, as writers, are no different. Thus, we adopt a stance of encouragement to let them know that we find their writing valuable, that we will honor them with feedback and keep pushing forward as they write, revise, and write some more.

Third, we adopt a stance of *celebration*. This is not the kind of stifled, perfunctory celebration that follows many students when they share their work in classes filled with polite claps and downcast eyes. Instead, in our efforts to build community and fully support writers, we structure response throughout the process and remind students that their work is about more than a grade. It is also about more than competition. We believe that the fact that you have written is, in and of itself, worth celebrating, and a reason to keep writing.

With these stances, we are not trying to be clichéd or trite. These are the overarching themes that emerged for us as we wrote the book, and you will see us return to them over and over again as we also connect to professional documents that guide us, the *Framework* and the *Professional Knowledge*.

Grounding Our Work

There are—in the research literature, practitioner-oriented journals, books, and blog posts, and from conference presentations and workshops—dozens if not hundreds of models of literacy learning from which we could draw our core beliefs about what it means to be a reader and writer, speaker and listener, viewer and producer of visual texts. From these numerous models, we would likely see similarities about the ways in which student agency is prized, that reading and writing happen for authentic purposes, and that assessment practices are more authentic and less punitive. These are themes that run through a shared vision of literacy learning that has come to be recognized in our field over the past three decades.

As noted above, both of us have found our professional homes with the National Writing Project (NWP) and the National Council of Teachers of English (NCTE), as well as with our local and state-level affiliates of these groups. We will return to these organizations and their impact on our lives throughout the book, though it is also important to note that we will talk about additional strategies for professional growth once we reach the conclusion. For the moment, we delve deeply into two documents produced by these organizations, the first in partnership with each other as well as with the Council of Writing Program Administrators, and the second produced by NCTE alone. While we know that we could draw from many other significant works offered by other constituent groups of NCTE—including the Conference on College Composition and Communication (CCCC) and the Two-Year College English Association (TYCA), among others—we limit our attention here to these two documents as a way to remain focused and concise.

We are also informed, for better and for worse, by the Common Core English Language Arts standards. The second decade of the twenty-first century began with the launch of these new standards in June of 2010, and state-level adoption of them occurred in much of the nation, including our home state of Michigan, over subsequent years. And while there are certainly many critics of the Common

Core and its prescriptive lists (e.g., Shannon, 2013), we do see their ideas expressed in the "capacities of the literate individual" (Common Core State Standards Initiative, n.d.) as being useful for discussions with our own writers. These capacities include:

- Independence, where students are "self-directed learners, effectively seeking out and using resources to assist them, including teachers, peers, and print and digital reference materials";
- A strong knowledge base gained "by engaging with works of quality and substance";
- A writer's stance with an ability to "adapt their communication in relation to audience, task, purpose, and discipline";
- The ability to comprehend and critique a variety of texts as "engaged and open-minded—but discerning—readers and listeners";
- A disposition toward logic and reasoning, being able to "cite specific evidence when offering an oral or written interpretation of a text";
- Using technology in thoughtful ways to "to enhance their reading, writing, speaking, listening, and language use," a point we return to in more detail below;
- And, finally, the ability to "seek to understand other perspectives and cultures through reading and listening" as well as "to communicate effectively with people of varied backgrounds."

Teachers send an empowering message when they show students that what is important to them, as writers, is also important to the teacher as someone who also writes and values good writing. The Common Core is not the be-all and end-all, and we recognize that the standards still generate a significant range of feelings among educators, parents, policy makers, and students themselves.

However, we still find that this list of capacities parallels what we believe about the teaching of writing and how we can frame our planning, teaching, and assessment. As professional teachers of writing, viewing standards as flexible opportunities we can explore—instead of as fixed concepts we "have" to teach—creates a new perspective.

From that perspective, we are able to offer writing invitations for students that can empower their learning, inspire their writing, and seek opportunities they view as authentic. Moreover, we contend that the Common Core ELA standards for writing, by and large, align with both of the professional documents—the *Framework* and *Professional Knowledge*—and we introduce them next.

The Framework for Success in Postsecondary Writing

Among the many policy documents, reports, curricular materials, journal articles, books, and other resources these organizations have produced, we are especially appreciative of their collaboration with the Council of Writing Program Administrators in the 2011 document, *The Framework for Success in Postsecondary Writing*. Its goal is straightforward: it "describes the rhetorical and twenty-first-century skills as well as habits of mind and experiences that are critical for college success" (p. 1).

The *Framework* provides a clear map to the moves that can create confident writers. It also recognizes that a variety of writing experiences will deepen and diversify how students perceive writing. Writing for personal joy includes goals, habits, and routines, each of which are linked to postsecondary writing habits of mind that share "ways of approaching learning that are both intellectual and practical and that will support students' success in a variety of fields and disciplines." In our writing lives, the habits of curiosity, openness, engagement, creativity, persistence, responsibility, flexibility, and metacognition all move us forward, especially when we choose the genre or mode of writing. It is not a unique experience but, rather, one that is common for writers entering into (and living in) the postsecondary world. The framework helps us as we plan, teach, and assess student writers.

At the core of the *Framework* is engagement. Not simply time on-task, this is about the time students are engaged with writing. It may seem a small, albeit nuanced, difference between being on-task and engaged, but the difference is striking. Students who play school well can be on-task by following the instructions of the teacher without being connected to the work they are doing, whereas when students are engaged, they are attuned to and care about improving a piece of writing as they work through ideas important to them.

Engagement is at the heart of student writer growth and learning. For students to see themselves as writers, they need to be immersed in the art of writing by seeing and hearing a variety of written texts. Equally important is for students to see a writer's process in action. When students see us, as writers, making these moves during our teaching demonstrations, they become aware of the inner workings of the craft. Furthermore, when they see the process of a teacher as writer, they undoubtedly will witness struggle and how to negotiate it.

The *Framework* provides the reminders that writers need to combat self-doubt and see writing as a way to learn, grow, and increase their sphere of knowledge. Troy shares these reminders with students at the beginning of the semester, and for Andy the habits of mind are prominently displayed on a bulletin board in the class-

BOX 1: "Executive Summary" from *The Framework for Success in Postsecondary Writing*

"Habits of mind" refers to ways of approaching learning that are both intellectual and practical and that will support students' success in a variety of fields and disciplines. The *Framework* identifies eight habits of mind essential for success in college writing:

- Curiosity – the desire to know more about the world;
- Openness – the willingness to consider new ways of being and thinking in the world;
- Engagement – a sense of investment and involvement in learning;
- Creativity – the ability to use novel approaches for generating, investigating, and representing ideas;
- Persistence – the ability to sustain interest in and attention to short- and long-term projects;
- Responsibility – the ability to take ownership of one's actions and understand the consequences of those actions for oneself and others;
- Flexibility – the ability to adapt to situations, expectations, or demands;
- Metacognition – the ability to reflect on one's own thinking as well as on the individual and cultural processes used to structure knowledge.

The *Framework* then explains how teachers can foster these habits of mind through writing, reading, and critical analysis experiences. These experiences aim to develop students':

- Rhetorical knowledge – the ability to analyze and act on understandings of audiences, purposes, and contexts in creating and comprehending texts;
- Critical thinking – the ability to analyze a situation or text and make thoughtful decisions based on that analysis, through writing, reading, and research;
- Writing processes – multiple strategies to approach and undertake writing and research;
- Knowledge of conventions – the formal and informal guidelines that define what is considered to be correct and appropriate, or incorrect and inappropriate, in a piece of writing;
- Abilities to compose in multiple environments – from using traditional pen and paper to electronic technologies.

room, becoming infused with day-to-day conversation. These are more directly applicable to students, whereas NCTE's *Professional Knowledge* document is aimed more directly at educators, which we explore next.

Professional Knowledge for the Teaching of Writing

The *Professional Knowledge for the Teaching of Writing* position statement includes ten "professional principles that guide effective teaching," which cover areas ranging from the teaching of grammar and conventions to the idea that "writing is a process" and can be used as a tool for thinking. The history of the document goes back to the early 2000s, when a subcommittee of NCTE's executive committee wrote a first version of this document: the *Beliefs about the Teaching of Writing*. The 2016 update acknowledges the increasingly ubiquitous role of technology as well as the impacts—positive and negative—of the Common Core. Acknowledging these "historically significant changes of recent years," the revised NCTE statement offers ten professional principles, as listed in Box 2.

BOX 2: Overarching Principles from the *Professional Knowledge for the Teaching of Writing*

In their guiding document, NCTE articulates ten principles for teachers to consider as they teach students how to write. Summarized here, they include:

- Writing grows out of many purposes.
- Writing is embedded in complex social relationships and their appropriate languages.
- Composing occurs in different modalities and technologies.
- Conventions of finished and edited texts are an important dimension of the relationship between writers and readers.
- Everyone has the capacity to write; writing can be taught; and teachers can help students become better writers.
- Writing is a process.
- Writing is a tool for thinking.
- Writing has a complex relationship to talk.
- Writing and reading are related.
- Assessment of writing involves complex, informed, human judgment.

Supporting the habits of mind for postsecondary success, NCTE's *Professional Knowledge* also provides ideas to help frame the conversations found in this book. To smooth the transition from high school to college, we agree that writing success is based on relationships formed through dialogue, not just through a list of tasks to be completed. For instance, we invite students to enter into text-centered conversations by using book clubs, one-on-one conferring while they read, project proposals, Pecha Kucha presentations (short, rapid-fire talks with slides advancing automatically every 20 seconds), guest blog-post publishing, and exploring digital mentor texts, among other tasks. We believe that creating the conditions for conversation is more important than tests and quizzes. We should assess in a way that is going to create confident writers—meaning a lot less with the red pen and a lot more with gentle nudges. We know that writing must be employed in a variety of ways, over time, and it is with this in mind that we use writing for a variety of purposes throughout any given class session, unit, or entire trimester.

Both the *Framework* and *Professional Knowledge* help us get closer to these goals. And, as we will explore next, so too does our work as teacher-writers. Before that, one other note about how we use the *Framework* and *Professional Knowledge* here. While many of the ideas presented are interwoven, and any one example of an assignment or student work may actually connect to multiple elements of each, we will throughout the book try to draw specific attention to one aspect of either the *Framework* or *Professional Knowledge*, as we do below.

BOX 3: Setting Up a Course Rich with Writing Opportunities

In the segment of *Professional Knowledge* on "Writing grows out of many purposes," one of the principles that teachers should understand is: "How to set up a course that asks students to write for varied purposes and audiences." While we know that classrooms and students differ, our hope in *Creating Confident Writers* is to provide our readers with innovative, flexible ideas that can, when combined with your own approaches, help set up a course that invites students to write for many different situations. These text boxes will help, quite literally, as we call out some of those ideas and connect them to the *Framework* and *Professional Knowledge*.

Being and Becoming: The Work of Teacher-Writers

While our book is about creating confidence in student writers, we contend that confidence begins with our own writing process.

Thus, another thread that ties the two of us together and fuels our work is that we both identify as teacher-writers. Drawing from a description that Troy and his colleagues shared in their book *Coaching Teacher-Writers*, Andy and Troy also believe that "the power of teachers' voices to build coalitions, to alter power relationships, and to advocate for policies and practices" is essential (Hicks, Whitney, Fredricksen & Zuidema, 2016, p. 131). While most English teachers will admit they are readers and that their identity as readers enables them to talk about books in nuanced and informed ways, we have found that it is less likely that those same English teachers will claim to be writers.

Those who do wear the identity of writer, like those who are avid readers, find their approach to writing and their interaction with student writers taking a different form. Teacher-writers become, in a sense, "authors in residence" in their own classrooms. They have an intimate relationship with a writing process that they have learned to negotiate. The experience that teacher-writers have with the complex and, at times, emotional underpinnings of writing creates an empathy for student writers who are working through their own processes.

Sadly, in many contexts, we know that teachers are not invited to see themselves as writers, nor to enact a writerly life. Directives are handed down from department chairs, curriculum directors, or other administrators like batons in a relay race nobody really wants to run. These overarching measures create a one-size-fits-all assembly line of education and of writing instruction. They have turned the joyful creative nature of learning to write into a series of tasks consisting of *read something, write an essay, get a grade, repeat.*

In many ways, teachers can feel hemmed in by these repetitive practices in the same way students do. Nonetheless, there are possibilities when teachers identify as writers. The life of a teacher-writer can take many forms. Some we know write merely for self, tending privately to their craft. Others maintain daily journals, participate in writing groups, and maintain blogs on topics of personal interest. Still others venture toward publishing in journals, poetry anthologies, and books. In our view, there is no right way to engage in writing as a teacher, yet we know that our conviction as writers can transfer to our students as they, too, find their way toward confidence.

We acknowledge that writing (and sharing one's writing) is a vulnerable experience. We encourage teachers to elevate the expectations we have of writing instruction by helping our students to embrace vulnerability, to seek authentic writing opportunities, and to tell their truths as writers. We must be willing to do this ourselves. As Christine Dawson argues in *The Teacher-Writer: Creating Writing Groups for Personal and Professional Growth*:

> *Considering teacher-writers through the lens of invention helps highlight their professional and personal knowledge and creativity, drawing attention to the multiple things they may invent: texts, writing practices, writing communities, and even identities as writers. (2016, p. 2, emphasis in original)*

While we understand and appreciate the fact that not all teachers of writing aspire to be teacher-writers, we do want to reiterate both here and in the rest of the book that, for both Andy and Troy, being writers and engaging in continuous acts of invention have become central parts of our pedagogy. The final chapter in the book provides many resources for growing and sustaining one's work as a teacher-writer.

Overview of Remaining Chapters

As the book progresses, we welcome you into an ongoing conversation about the nature of students as writers, the role of standards and professional guidelines, and the many stresses that play out in our writing instruction at both the high school and the college level. Each chapter looks at a primary aspect of our instructional decision making—inviting you, as a writing teacher, to be part of this dialogue. Here is a brief overview of what we plan to cover in each of the subsequent chapters, in which we will include examples of assignments, student work, assessments, and reflections, and you can continue the conversation at #creatingconfidentwriters.

Each chapter begins with a quote from a student; we then provide an anecdote from Andy's or Troy's classroom, bringing the chapter's topic into focus. From there, we name the approach that underlies this pedagogy and move into a number of specific activities, illustrated with student examples. Each chapter will close with questions and an invitation to our readers to consider the implications of what we have shared for your own teaching practice. We have structured the book around our three stances—invitation, encouragement, and celebration—and there will be echoes of these ideas throughout. With that in mind, we offer the following in the remaining sections and chapters.

In Section 1, *Invite*, we present two chapters showing how we adopt this stance in our classrooms. Chapter 1, aptly titled "Offering Invitations," introduces some strategies for breaking the ice and letting students know that we want to learn about their passions, questions, and needs. Chapter 2, "Setting Goals," shows how we help students frame their work for the trimester/semester, using tools like portfolios and paper proposals. Throughout this section, we demonstrate the ways in which an invitational stance can help students see that their voice is welcomed and that, while we have high expectations, we are also flexible and supportive in our efforts to create confident writers.

In Section 2, *Encourage*, we share three chapters. We use Chapter 3 for "Exploring Mentor Texts," moving beyond traditional essays and thinking broadly about what it means for students to write, speak, and visually present their work in a variety of modes and media. In Chapter 4, we delve more deeply into the role of reading in our students' lives, exploring how "Responding to Reading" can move beyond the traditional book report. As we close this segment and reaffirm our goals to create confident writers, we offer Chapter 5, "Revising and Resubmitting." As core components in an ongoing approach to teaching writing and supporting writers, we show how feedback is central to our pillar of providing encouragement.

In Section 3, we turn to *Celebrate*. In Chapter 6, we demonstrate ways that students are "Reflecting on Growth." More than just turning in a final portfolio, this chapter shows the deliberate ways in which we encourage metacognition and celebrate the skills that our students have learned, the risks they have taken, and the products they have composed.

Finally, we offer a brief conclusion in which we describe ways for sustaining your growth with a personal learning network, offering some suggestions for how we each stay connected to other teacher-writers who, like us, are working to create confident writers through invitation, encouragement, and celebration. In turn, we invite you to become part of the ongoing dialogue. As a reminder, we offer an authors' website for this book <hickstro.org/confidentwriters>, and we invite you to engage with us via social media, especially Twitter, where you can find Andy (@aschoenborn) and Troy (@hickstro). You can also use the hashtag #creatingconfidentwriters.

Also, we pause here to note that for all student work and quotes used in the text, we have taken the liberty of correcting small typographical errors. While we recognize that many educators and writers would want to stay true to exactly what was written in the student's text and indicate errors with a "*sic*," we felt that these few instances could be distracting for readers of this book. Across all instances of student work, there were very few mistakes to begin with, we took it upon ourselves to make these few minor corrections.

To sum up, we approach the task of creating confident writers with many emotions, and we acknowledge the feelings of joy and sorrow that teaching can bring. We end with one final caveat. Though the examples seem pristine, the stories impossibly perfect, we struggle, too. Most of the time, we (and our students) are impassioned and eager. Sometimes, we (and our students) are overwhelmed and even a bit nervous. Usually, our emotions (and, again, our students' emotions) land somewhere between these two extremes. We are pragmatic about our work, knowing that some students will embrace our approach and others would much prefer to "play the game of school" (Fried, 2005), keeping with more traditional assignments and expectations. This causes some friction, and we will try to acknowledge those tensions in the chapters ahead. Still, on the whole, we are satisfied that our students are becoming more and more confident from our first moments in class right up to the point they share their final work.

Our hope is that, in *Creating Confident Writers*, you will be able to explore this range of experiences and emotions, too. Let's begin.

CREATING CONFIDENT WRITERS

SECTION 1

INVITE

CHAPTER 1

Offering Invitations

*"None of my English teachers have ever
really pushed enjoying and having a relationship with writing, rather just get good at it."*

—Evan Grossnickle, Mt. Pleasant High School (MPHS)

Offering Invitations Creates Confident Writers by . . .

- Providing opportunities for innovative genres and authentic audiences;
- Introducing generative patterns of peer response;
- Balancing a sense of structure with possibilities for exploration;
- Demonstrating flexible aspects of writing that can contribute to an author's craft.

There is a perception, for most students in high school and college, that the words they write are valued as long as they meet standards, create acceptable data, and produce good grades. Perhaps it is the nature of our current educational system. Perhaps it is the result of standardized testing. Perhaps it is just the way it is for the majority of students. In this scenario, students are infrequently invited to write in ways meaningful to them, which understandably trends toward an apathetic view of writing.

As teachers, we make dozens of instructional decisions, both large and small, every day. We understand and live with the challenge of meeting curricular, state, and national standards. Often, like our students, we are tasked with producing results in spite of what we know fuels our passion to write. Rarely are we afforded the time to ask the deeper, more substantive questions about what guides the decision-making process. What drives us? Though there is never enough time in the day, both of us agree that slowing down, periodically, to ask these questions is crucial in our efforts to grow as educators. Equally, if not more, important are the decisions we make in our classrooms to slow down and invite students to see for themselves the writer's voice that they each have hidden within. We need to shine a light on the value their words bring to the world.

Be it academic, practical, creative, or digital, writing plays a role in schooling—that much we all agree. The specific role it plays may vary considerably from class-room to classroom and, as John Warner reminds us, it "requires a prioritization of values" in which we ask ourselves, "What conditions and experiences help learners improve and make them eager to keep coming back to learn more?" (2018, p. 108). This chapter focuses on a set of conditions and experiences that we contend keep writers coming back for more: invitations.

By definition, invitations are a "request to be present or participate" *(Merriam-Webster Online Dictionary*, n.d.). They are intentional moves we make in the class-room in an effort to invite students to present themselves in powerful and often vulnerable ways. We believe that, if a writer is to write, they must be willing to tell their truth even in the face of potential criticism. The practices found here and throughout *Creating Confident Writers* promote the resiliency found in the heart of every confident writer. To that end, we wonder, as teachers, when and how we pro-vide our students with genuine opportunities to be in the moment and engage fully with their own writing.

BOX 1.2: Writing Grows Out of Many Purposes

According to NCTE's guiding principles, "In order to provide high-quality writing opportunities for all students, teachers need to understand . . . how to set up a course that asks students to write for varied purposes and audiences" (2016). Though we know that it can be challenging to contin-ually innovate in our assignment design, we must help students find new readers and strive for a goal beyond earning a grade. One resource to discover many audiences and purposes for writing is Traci Gardner's 2011 book, *Designing Writing Assignments*, and especially Chapter 4, "Defining New Tasks for Standard Writing Activities," available as an open-access e-book from this chapter's page on the authors' website.

We invite you, here and throughout the book, to join us in collegial conversation about approaches that lend themselves to writing invitations. When teaching writing, we consider these questions:

- Through our words and actions, do we invite student voice and perspective into our classroom as a way to honor the writers as well as the words we are immersed in?
- Through the opportunities for writing we create, do we ask students to take risks by sharing their emotions as well as their intellect?
- By creating generative spaces, do we encourage dialogue, debate, reflection, and praise?
- Over the course of a trimester or semester, do we provide opportunities for students to develop writing goals for themselves?

These are difficult questions, ones that we wrestle with each day and that, to be clear, we never know for sure that we are getting right. Yet, to create confident writers, we must wrestle with them and, in doing so, generate a frame for thinking, reading, and writing in our classrooms.

Creating Confidence from the First Moments

The opportunity to provide invitations can only occur when we have created the conditions for students to feel comfortable and safe. These conditions begin from the first moments of class with invitations for students to be immersed in language. We believe there are many ways to create classroom environments that honor both students and the written word. You may already have a process that works for you that stays true to your authentic self, and we encourage you to embrace it. As a brief example, however, let's see how Andy offers invitations on the first day of the trimester.

As students begin to settle, he dims the lights, unmutes the LCD projector, and plays Shane Koyczan and Hannah Epperson's rendition of the poem "Remember How We Forgot" (EveryDayMusicTV, 2013), launching students into an immediate, immersive literacy experience (video link on the authors' website). The closing lines, in particular, are a powerful call to action: "And our story starts: / 'We were here.'" (Koyczan, n.d.). After the spoken word poem, Andy introduces a pattern of response that will be reiterated throughout the year. "Snap your fingers along with me to honor the words we just heard," he says. Students, often reluctantly, join in, until the room is filled with more enthusiasm than trepidation.

Once this initial response has subsided, he shares his thoughts on the poem:

"Language is a celebration of literacy, life, and experience when we are vulnerable enough to perceive it as such." Then, as the remaining snaps die down, he continues.

"How many of you speak a second language?" A few hands go up and he gestures toward a student.

"I'm sure you know this then: what is the best way to learn a second language?"

The student offers a hesitant response: "You need to speak it."

"Yes! That's it! You need to speak it!"

He continues speaking to the class and asks, "Do you know what works best when learning to speak a second language?" The class pauses, not quite sure how to answer.

He waits a moment, then continues.

"I think that each of you know the answer because each of you, at one time, had to learn to speak a language. How did you learn to speak your primary language?"

A second student answers with a bit more bravado.

"We just did. We were immersed in it and had others, like parents, who encouraged us."

"Right! Immersion is the key to getting better at anything! And what keeps you coming back?"

The same student chimes in again. "When we are encouraged to try again, and when others are patient with us."

"Right again! Aren't those the learning experiences that stick with you the most?"

A few students nod in agreement and yet another student raises her hand.

"Yeah," she begins. "Those are the times when I actually want to try, because I know someone cares."

Andy, who has been moving around the room, moves closer to this student and says, "Isn't that interesting? I want to know more about that. Please, tell me more."

And the conversation continues from there.

From the first moments, Andy invites students to participate in a dramatic literacy experience. The Koyczan poem is one that holds many truths, and it sets the tone for a classroom experience that is different from one that many students have encountered before. When the spoken word poem comes to a close, Andy models genuine appreciation for the words they just heard and invites students to snap along with him in a simple protocol of appreciation that will carry students through the duration of the course. Before his students even notice it, they find themselves in an authentic community of learners who are invited and encouraged to celebrate words in many forms.

Structured Routines that Invite Writing Habits

As we consider the many ways in which we can offer invitations to our students, a precursor to doing so is establishing a routine. Although many educators hold on to the notion that the "reading and writing workshop" approach is for primary grades, its flexible application puts secondary students at the center of their learning. From our youngest students in kindergarten up through graduate school, reading and writing workshops can be used as an effective structure to foster the habits of mind for literacy. It is a structure that honors the work of a writer.

Nancie Atwell, a writing workshop pioneer, is always open to ways that will help her students discover the writer within. In her book *In the Middle*, she describes the workshop approach as a stance, stating:

I knew I wanted to try to create an environment conducive to writing: a writing workshop, with plenty of time to write and plenty of oppor-

tunities for choice, response, and publication . . . I'm striving for the fluid, subtle, exhilarating balance that allows me to function in my classroom as a listener and a teller, an observer and an actor, a collab-orator and a critic and a cheerleader. (1998, pp. 20–21)

We agree with Atwell—and with countless other advocates of a reading and writing workshop approach—and we see our roles as facilitators of writing instruction. Workshop instruction features predictable structures, small moves to build community, and safe spaces for talk. Andy and Troy accomplish these goals in slightly different ways, given their different teaching contexts. At the same time, our practices shift, flow, and pivot as we gain experience learning with new students each year. In short, there is no one right way to incorporate a reading and writing workshop in your classroom, and we recognize and respect the need for differences.

For Andy, the daily schedule includes a 72-minute class period found in a typical American high school on block schedules and trimesters. For Troy, the college schedule is vastly different; he sees his students for only about 2.5 hours per week, sometimes on two separate days, and sometimes in a large afternoon/evening block. Still, each workshop consists of a few tried-and-true characteristics in the traditional model: a quick write; independent reading time; a read-aloud (poetry, book, or mentor text in the genre under study); a mini-lesson to teach writing craft, techniques, and strategies; significant time for writing practice; writing conferences; and whole-class sharing. While these are the hallmarks of a writing workshop, it is common (and expected) that teachers find ways to modify the workshop for their own purposes.

Regardless of the workshop structure, students should find themselves immersed in literacy; this involves responsive craft lessons, reading/writing choice, conferences, and sharing of progress toward goals. In their book, *180 Days: Two Teachers and the Quest to Engage and Empower Adolescents* (2018), Kelly Gallagher and Penny Kittle share their modified approaches based on their individual teaching situations. Gallagher and Kittle (pp. 26–27) add three key ideas when setting up an everyday structure for these practices:

- This structure is not grade specific.
- Students control the pace and focus of their work during 75 percent of each class.
- The sequence and timing of moves in a workshop are malleable.

TABLE 1.1: Possible Structures for Reading and Writing Workshop

Gallagher's Classroom – 53 Minutes Every Day	Kittle's Classroom – 80 Minutes Every Other Day	Schoenborn's Classroom – 72 Minutes Every Day
• Book talk (2 min) • Silent reading (10 min) • Notebook writing (10 min) • Mini-lesson, mentor text, or assignment instructions (8 min) • Workshop time (20 min) • Final sharing (remaining time)	• Book talk (4 min) • Silent reading (15 min) • Notebook writing (10 min) • Mini-lesson, mentor text, or assignment instructions (10–15 min) • Workshop time (30–35 min) • Final sharing (remaining time)	• Poetry/book talk (5 min) • Silent reading or creative writing (20 min) • Mini-lesson, mentor text, or assignment instructions (10–15 min) • Workshop time (30–35 min) • Final sharing (remaining time)

Source: Compiled from Kelly Gallagher and Penny Kittle's book, 180 Days: Two Teachers and the Quest to Engage and Empower Adolescents, *and Andy Schoenborn's Class Schedule*

Andy has modeled his classroom routines in a similar manner and has modified the writing workshop structure to work for his needs. Working within the frame of a College Board–approved syllabus and the curricular demands of his district, he has found an everyday workshop structure that works for him. He strikes a balance between independent reading and creative writing by incorporating them every other day. Table 1.1 shows how Andy's schedule compares to Gallagher's and Kittle's.

For Troy, the schedule is a bit different depending on the day and the writing task at hand. Teaching in 75-minute blocks, whether on two days of the week or in one afternoon/evening stretch, he typically divides it so one class per week is devoted fully to workshop time (mini-lesson, writing and conferring, peer response, and sharing) while the other session is devoted to other activities, which could include specific writing-to-learn tasks, mini-lectures, group activities, or student presentations. Without a doubt, he feels the crunch of offering students the time and space to write about topics and in genres of their own choosing, yet he still pushes against the urge to cram more "content" into the class. For Troy, 75 percent of class time is a bit too much to turn over to workshop time, and 50 percent is probably closer to the norm for him.

BOX 1.3: Everyone Has the Capacity to Write

Inviting students to write is not just something that happens, like magic, when students are presented with a prompt and asked to write. Instead, as NCTE notes, "[i]n order to provide high-quality writing opportunities for all students, teachers need to understand . . . how to construct social structures that support independent work." In this sense, the ways that we welcome students to connect with one another, to listen to each other as writers, matters. The activities described in this chapter help build connections and community.

Conversation Invites Confident Writing

In addition to the workshop routine itself, structuring ways for students to talk with one another is crucial, too. Embedded in the writing workshop are purposeful moments to generate talk and reflect on writing while it is in process. In order to move writers forward, there are phrases designed to center the conversation around the writing and the choices of the author. In his book, *Choice Words: How Our Language Affects Children's Learning* (2004), Peter Johnston describes these phrases as a "Family of Responses" (pp. 23–26) that are meant to develop positive student writer identities, develop writer-created goals, and internalize reflection on writing, two of which include: "How does it make you feel to have written a piece like this?" and "How have you changed as a writer?"

These questions send the message that writers are in control of their process and that the teacher is there to provide perspective as a reader. These micro-goals and affirmations help student writers consider the moves they make in a text. In addition, they open up authentic conversations about writing as each student needs it. Additionally, there are a number of phrases that we have brought into our own teaching practice, all designed to build confidence in students:

- "Did anyone notice what [name] said? It is interesting because . . ."
- "That is a great point! I appreciate what [name] said, because . . ."
- "I had never thought of it that way before, [name]. Tell me more."
- "That's brilliant, [name]! Do you mind if I write that down?"

- "What a powerful moment, [name]. Thank you for being vulnerable and trusting us."
- "Wow! I've never thought of it that way, [name]. I appreciate that you offered it up for us to consider."

In-process, reflective talk about writing can and should find space in our teaching; it can be scheduled around the writer during conferring time, or with a whole group of writers during mini-lesson instruction. With these routines established, the opportunities for deeper, even more meaningful writing can begin through invitations like the ones we explore next.

Suffice it to say, when teachers structure their class sessions in predictable, yet flexible, ways, they, paradoxically, actually free themselves from a lock-step approach to teaching. The routines of the day and the week provide flexibility that honors the student. Our goal is not to cover everything in the curriculum; instead, it is to respond to student writers where they are in their process. This requires teachers to make small moves that have a big impact, moves that can happen in a workshop structure and, over time, can help to create confident writers. With these routines established, we can then move into the work of writing.

BOX 1.4: Writing Has a Complex Relationship to Talk

NCTE acknowledges that we must develop "[w]ays of setting up and managing student talk in partnerships and groups." With the types of questions provided here, teachers can model for students the kinds of interactions that they would expect of their students while engaged in conversation with one another. We sometimes even go so far as to provide students with "sentence starters" to ensure that they are engaging in productive talk when responding to one another.

Writing Activities that Offer Invitations

With the activities described in the next three sections, we show how our first principle, invitation, works as a way to get students started, ensuring that their voices are part of the conversation, both in print and as part of our ongoing classroom dialogue.

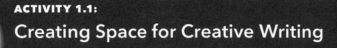

ACTIVITY 1.1:
Creating Space for Creative Writing

Perhaps one of our most important jobs as writing teachers is to help our writers understand that literacy is much more than reading, researching, and academic writing. For many students, the only real changes they see in their ELA and composition courses over the years are that the mechanical demands become stricter (with specific attention to MLA, APA, or other style guides) and the papers get longer. It is an unfortunate reality that turns many of those same students away from writing or, worse yet, forces them to see school-based prose as the only kind of writing that counts.

With that in mind, we need to welcome student writers with invitations they are able to choose. Providing a choice for students in topic, genre, or mode of writing increases ownership of their learning. In addition, it helps them to see value in their work. For Andy, this means biweekly opportunities for in-class creative writing and employing Natalie Goldberg's "List of Writing Rules" from *Writing Down the Bones: Freeing the Writer Within* (2010, p. 8). These opportunities produce powerful moments for students to explore their own ideas. As Goldberg advises, Andy asks writers to "Keep your hand moving"; "Don't cross out"; and, metaphorically, to "Go for the jugular." Students choose to keep their writing in a writer's notebook or create a Google Doc, both of which are for their eyes only. When students are given inspiration, choice, and time to write, they soon awaken the muse they did not know was lying dormant within them.

When it comes to quantity, we agree with Kelly Gallagher who says that, "as a general rule of thumb, students are asked to write four times more than [we] can physically assess" (2006, p. 53). Increasing the volume of writing students are expected to do increases their time on the page and, therefore, increases their time thinking like writers. Choosing low-risk writing invitations helps students become comfortable with the page, their thoughts, and their writing. We look for assessment that reduces the writer's time spent listening to their inner critic and increases time spent in celebration of their ideas as they learn.

At the midterm and end-of-term, time designated for creative writing shifts from generating writing to choosing one piece of writing that surprised them. Students learn revision techniques during short mini-lessons and reenvision a piece they would like to submit for a grade in their portfolio. In this credit/no credit assessment, students are asked to meet five criteria. Their piece must include a summative image, a title, a piece of writing suitable for publication, "words from the author" in which they share their inspiration (VanDerwater, 2017), and a significant "revision decision" (Anderson & Dean, 2014), explaining a rhetorical move they made in the piece (which will be explored in more detail in Chapter 5).

Incorporating the freedom of creative writing gives students the chance to spread their writer's wings. They write for the sake of writing, and although Andy offers writing prompts, he always begins creative writing time by saying, "I don't care *what* you write; I just care *that* you write, creatively." When students prepare to submit their work, he reminds them that since he asks them "to be vulnerable in their writing and write from their soul," if their pieces meet the five criteria listed above, they will earn full credit because "whose soul is worth any less than one hundred percent? No one's."

Invitations for students to write creatively during classroom routines often produce impressive results. Consider these stanzas of Kennedy Griffin's poem, "Everything But Us," which shares her perspective on race and culture (as noted in the Introduction, links to samples of student work and assignment templates are available on the authors' website: <hickstro.org/confidentwriters>.

As an African American student in a predominantly white school, Kennedy had been exploring questions about identity based on her interest with #BlackLivesMatter. She seized the creative writing opportunities given in Andy's class to dig into and explore the tensions she experiences in her life. In particular, she feels that "everything from our food to our headwraps and hair techniques" have been appropriated. While she had not cited a specific example of this happening at school, she was able to share many examples from current events and pop culture. Also, as she reflected, she makes an effort in the final stanza to frame a question "meant to push the reader deep into thought" by asking "So why is it, / That these people who claim to love everything about us, / Seem to love everything about us, / But us?"

Kennedy, having had the opportunity for some independent and creative writing, used this writing invitation to explore issues of identity. For her, and for many students, the opportunity to do this kind of writing, thinking, and reflecting is not often found in a typical English classroom, which

**BOX 1.5: A Selection from Kennedy Griffin's Poem,
"Everything But Us"**

They love our headwraps,
The way the do-rag's elegant colors and prints
Curve and caress their way around our hair.

They love our hair,
The way our kinks, curls, and coils
Frame our elegant faces with such pride.

They love our faces,
The way the chocolate melts into our eyes
And drips down along our arms and stomachs.

They love our food,
The way the lingering taste
Of Creole and soul food
Makes their skin seize with satisfaction.

They love our skin,
"Sunkissed is never the right word," they say,
Infatuated with how the melanin encases
Our muscles and tendons and smiles.

They love the sound of us,
The way our words and notes curl
Around the saxophones and double bass

So why is it,
That these people who claim to love everything about us
Seem to love everything about us,
But us?

usually focuses on thematic essays. In thinking about the habits of mind, Kennedy certainly expressed creativity and flexibility.

As we think about additional ways students like Kennedy can extend their thinking, we are reminded of Amy Ludwig VanDerwater, mentioned briefly above, who discusses the power of poetry in her book *Poems Are Teachers* (2017). Here she argues that "poems teach us how to write. Any-

BOX 1.6: Creativity and Flexibility

Integrating creative writing into his classroom routines invited both Kennedy and Andy's other students to "use methods that are new to [her] to investigate questions, topics, and ideas" (5) as well as offering students the flexibility to "reflect on choices made in light of context, purpose, and audience" (5), both habits of mind from the *Framework*. In particular, this experience pushed Kennedy to explore an emerging rhetorical knowledge of poetry in order to "contribute, through writing, [her] own ideas and opinions about a topic to an ongoing conversation" (6), ideas also drawn from the *Framework*.

thing." Kennedy took the opportunity during creative writing time to run with this power, using the flexibility afforded by the prompt, and wrote about her experiences in a manner that, up to that point, she had not felt comfortable expressing in a traditional essay format. VanDerwater, and many others who advocate for poetry in the classroom—such as Fletcher (2013, 2017), Heard (2014), Romano (2000), and Bomer (2016)—give us, as teachers, permission to bring poetry into the classroom not just as a one-off unit but, rather, on a regular basis. By creating this celebration of words each and every day, Andy inspires confidence in his students. More resources are available on VanDerwater's website, linked from the authors' website page for this chapter.

ACTIVITY 1.2:
Trending Topics

In his TED Talk, "How Great Leaders Inspire Action" (2009), linked on the website, Simon Sinek makes the claim that all inspiring leaders and organizations globally think about the world differently. Most of us know what we do and how we do it, but rarely do we know why we do it. The people and groups who inspire us think in the opposite way. They focus first on why they aim to do something, then how they will do it, and, finally, what it is they are doing. Sinek calls this mindset "the Golden Circle," and it works quite well for creating writing invitations.

To write well, authors need two things: purpose and audience. In the school setting, helping student writers fulfill these needs in authentic ways can be challenging. We have found that a sincere invitation for students to find their purpose for writing, encouraging them to be vulnerable, and celebrating when they share helps them find their passion to write well. It is our goal, in writing workshops, to be responsive to the passions of our students. In doing so, we encourage our writers to dig into the heart of their why.

In an inquiry-based manner, Andy jump-starts students' thinking with a question: *What are the topics trending in your life?* Answers to this question are usually based on current events or topics students are wrestling with. He leads students through a process of sharing topics and narrowing down which ones seem to resonate the most. When Andy asked this question at the midpoint of the 2018–19 school year, the topics he received were layered with emotional weight. These topics in Table 1.2 are similar to polls of other youth, many of whom feel leery of their own college-readiness (YouthTruth, 2017), mental health (Interagency Working Group on Youth Programs, n.d.), and concerns about social justice issues (Flannery, 2014).

TABLE 1.2: Topics Trending in the Lives of Students in the 2018–19 School Year

#MeToo	Free Speech	Mental Illness
Poverty	LGBTQ+	Body Positivity
Gender Roles	Diversity	#BlackLivesMatter

Source: Student Generated List from Andy Schoenborn's Classroom

He asks students to think about themselves as readers, encouraging them to share what pulls them into a text. Their collective response is usually something to the effect that "it was relatable." Authors draw them in by letting them in on portions of their lives (or their characters' lives) that usually stay hidden. Andy's students understand that authors need not be confessional in their work but, to use their phrase, "they need to be real." He talks with them about what it means to be "real" and discovers that it happens when authors take risks in their writing, exposing weaknesses and vulnerability.

After the discussion, Andy gives everyone a sticky note and asks them to draw a large heart in the middle of the paper. He asks them to write the topic that touched them most at the top of the note. Inside the heart, he asks them to do what they expect from authors they admire: be vulnerable. To demonstrate his investment, Andy shares his experience with mental illness, specifically depression. If he expects students to dig deep, he has to be willing to be vulnerable with them, or else run the risk of seeming disingenuous.

When it is time for students to write their personal whys, they embrace the challenge. Students write about personal struggles with body image, about living with mental illness like clinical depression and living with loved ones struggling with bipolar disorder. Students dig into ideas about how the world views those who identify with the LGBTQ+ community. Again, from a recent AP Literature class, we can see the anonymous contributions in Figure 1.1, including:

- "I want to be respected."
- "I chose the topic of mental illness because I struggled with depression for the past three years. Being diagnosed made me more interested in the topic."
- "Mental illness is something I struggle w/ every day. Many of my friends also deal w/ it. I have issues recognizing my own."
- "As a male w/ different interests than a majority of my peers, I have experienced toxic masculinity."
- "Depression + suicidal thoughts run in my family."

Once students have come to terms with their why, they move into a deeper discussion of how they would explore their chosen topic. They dig deep. Tom Newkirk insists, "[a]ll writing is personal. That is, to be effective the writer has to locate some personal stake in it; otherwise the process is self-alienating" (2017, p. 149). For Andy's students, that means they are invited to navigate the heart of their why—or, more concisely, their truth.

Sharing a personal truth is difficult, even in the most comfortable of environments, and that challenge is amplified in the classroom. Though he does not ask them to be confessional in their writing or demand that they

FIGURE 1.1: The Heart of Our Why Sticky Note Activity

share their answers orally with the class, Andy does invite them to reflect in writing their personal connection to their topic.

With his students, Andy works to share some books that fit with the topics. Keeping with student interest and agency, they chose selections from YA books, classic literature, memoir, and poetry. Andy pairs topical texts with students, determining whether they work in a four-person book club, in trios, pairs, or individually. In addition to knowing how they are going to explore their topic (book pairings), he uses Kylene Beers and Bob Probst's "Book, Head, Heart" framework (2017) to help them connect with the books, a topic we explore more in Chapter 4, "Responding to Reading."

In the context of creating confident writers, an invitation to be open reminds us of Sarah Rose Cavanagh's work *The Spark of Learning* (2016), in which she asserts that "choosing activities, readings, and assignments that are interesting, self-relevant, emotionally evocative, and/or deeply relevant . . . may be the most powerful organizing principle you have as a teacher" (p. 212). Indeed, for our students, there is power knowing you are not alone.

BOX 1.7: Openness and Engagement

Telling their truths and being vulnerable requires openness, especially if we want students to engage in what the *Framework* suggests when they "examine their own perspectives to find connections with the perspectives of others" (4) as well as to "make connections between their own ideas and those of others" (4). They see the ways in which trending topics are part of a broader dialogue and, in return, are more likely to add their own voice. They deepen their rhetorical knowledge in order to "contribute, through writing, their own ideas and opinions about a topic to an ongoing conversation" (6).

Although Andy is careful to remind students to share only what they are comfortable with, the practice of digging into their *why* moves them beyond surface-level conversations. In addition, with multiple opportunities over the weeks of the trimester, grouping students under the umbrella of trending topics creates intimate communities that are centered around a common text. These micro-communities begin with the veils of vulnerability lifted just enough to connect members in meaningful ways to their topics, and to each other.

ACTIVITY 1.3:
Digital Identity Narratives

In Troy's college composition classes, as students begin a semester-long exploration of how personal, academic, and professional lives intersect in digital spaces, they encounter their first major project: the digital identity narrative, or the "Digital ID." Adapted from his colleague at the University of Rhode Island, Stephanie West-Puckett (n.d.), and built on many years of teaching students and other educators how to create digital stories (Lambert, 2010), Troy's goals for the Digital ID project are to help students explore the different "selves" that they have brought to college, zeroing in on one or two of these particular identities and creating a brief, 3–5 minute video that demonstrates students' emerging understanding of who they are and who they are becoming.

Borrowing from the assignment overview that West-Puckett and her URI colleagues have created, Troy poses the following questions to students at the beginning of the project, inviting them to consider the various identities they bring with them to college:

- What does it mean to be X?
- How do you know? How did you learn?
- How has that identity been shaped by cultural influences or different kinds of media?
- How has that identity shaped your life, life choices, health and well-being, or success as a student?
- How has your perception or experience of that identity changed over time?
- What should others know about your experience of being X, especially as it relates to your relationship with technology and media?

Over three weeks, students move through a series of activities where they create an initial online profile, review the profiles of others, analyze their rhetorical choices, view and deconstruct an existing digital identity narrative, and then prepare their own storyboard and script. Using whatever tool is most comfortable for them and available on the device they own, Troy coaches students through the process of moving from script and storyboard into video production. Students may use Adobe Spark, iMovie, Windows Movie Maker, or even open-source tools such as Open Shot (links are available on this chapter's page on the authors' website). In that process, students also learn a bit about copyright and are introduced to the concept of "transformative" fair use. Additionally, students are shown ways to find images, video clips, music tracks, and sound effects that may be in the public domain or are available for use under a Creative Commons license.

As they compose their projects, students bring their own unique perspectives and experiences to the screen. Media literacy scholar Renee

Hobbs, in her book *Create to Learn*, describes such a personal video in the following manner:

> *The video essay often relies on a complex relationship between language, image, and sound. The viewer must gather up the elements, listen, and look with the heart, to grasp the film's true meaning. Words don't capture the complexity—neither does sound or music or images. But when combined together, something magical happens. (2017, p. 192)*

As part of this complex composing process, students prepare a "rough draft" of their video and bring it to class to share for peer review. For that particular review, Troy invites them to consider the intersection of their own writing/narration, the strategic use of images and video clips, as well as any additional media or sound effects that their classmates have added.

In the example below, one of Troy's students, Julia, demonstrates how she has come to understand her family's experience as immigrants to America (2018). Her parents, originally from the Netherlands, relocated to America just after being married. Through family photos, maps from *Wiki-*

FIGURE 1.2: Screenshots from Julia's Digital Identity Narrative
pedia, images and video clips captured on her smartphone, and time-lapse

BOX 1.8: Persistence and Metacognition

For the majority of Troy's students, producing a digital video was a new task. Like her classmates, Julia demonstrated persistence as she worked to, as the *Framework* describes, "follow through, over time, to complete tasks, processes, or projects" (5) while harnessing a metacognitive stance to "connect choices [she] made in texts to audiences and purposes for which texts are intended" (5). This ability to move through a flexible writing process was important for all students as they adapted to new genres, new technologies, and expectations for writing that, for many, were outside of what they had experienced in high school.

pedia, images and video clips captured on her smartphone, and time-lapse sequence of her own work as a painter, Julia provides her viewers with a unique perspective on a contemporary—and controversial—issue, demonstrating the many ways in which the American dream is still alive and well, despite political rhetoric that would make people think otherwise.

Like Julia, each of Troy's students produced a compelling digital identity narrative, introducing themselves to their classmates in new—and sometimes surprising—ways. On the day that the class viewed the narratives together, there were rounds of applause, punctuated by some gasps, some laughs, and some tears. As Julia noted in her final reflection, "within that project, I had to learn to balance the different elements of pictures, text, video, and music to accurately and aesthetically portray my identities."

This invitation served as a way for students to better understand their own goals for pursuing higher education, explore the process of multi-modal composition, and gain confidence in their first semester as college writers. And, as Julia summarized her ideas about the many ways she worked on digital writing over the semester, "knowing how to incorporate other media into projects makes information and learning much more interesting by breaking up text and thinking critically about new and innovative ways to portray information."

In our experience, invitations require teachers who are willing to lead the way. As teacher-writers, we must choose to be our genuine and authentic selves in the classroom from the very first moments. If we are interested in creating confident writers, it behooves us to share our writing practices and vulnerabilities as we invite our students to do the same. It is here we recognize your value as a teacher-writer and invite you to embrace the writing invitations you offer your students.

Conclusion

From the first day of class, and up through the point at which they are sharing their words with the world, we both aim to honor the hearts of writers. The ways in which we structure the reading/writing workshops—even in AP Lit or a college composition classroom—allows students opportunities to explore pertinent topics, take risks with their writing, and begin to identify as writers.

We both push back against notions of what college-ready or college-level writing "is" or "should be," encouraging writers to break rules that they may think they should follow: never using "I," steering clear of the personal, and only writing in stilted, academic prose. There will be time for those kinds of writing and rules before the end of the semester, but the first invitations into writing in both Andy's and Troy's classrooms are ones that open doors rather than closing them.

So it is in this final segment of each chapter that we aim to open doors, to push your thinking. We know that teachers have their own teaching styles as well as their own personalities and preferences. And, of course, we know that all educators want to welcome students, in their own ways, to be part of a classroom community and to participate fully as readers and writers. Yet we also know, both from large-scale studies (such as those cited above) and from our own experiences, that many students still feel disconnected.

At the end of each chapter, we leave readers with a series of questions, considering opportunities for renewing our own approach to the use of "invitations" in our own writing classrooms:

- In what ways do you offer invitations to your students as readers and writers, in ways both small and large?
- How might you encourage students to "find their truth" or "get to the

heart of their why" by encouraging choice in topic, genre, and audience for writing?

- What opportunities might exist for more expressive writing, including poetry, that could enhance and extend conversations about the texts your students are reading?
- What additional digital writing opportunities could you offer to students as a way to explore their identities, their interests, and their goals?

CHAPTER 2

Setting Goals

"The way the class is set up in terms of making individual goals and pushing ourselves to achieve these goals was exactly what I needed."

—**Kayleigh Reilly, MPHS**

Setting Goals Creates Confident Writers by . . .

- Acknowledging who they are as writers, including their skills and interests, helping them envision where they would like to be;
- Empowering writers to get in touch with their personal writing purposes;
- Engaging in regular routines that build and maintain reading and writing momentum;
- Strengthening a writer's sense of investment or involvement.

We've all felt it. The overwhelming power of the blank page or screen, pen at the ready or cursor blinking, waiting for us to begin. Our students, even the most capable and motivated, sometimes feel that sense of paralysis, trying to figure out what they are going to say, how they are going to say it, and, in the end, whether or not their words will bring meaning to other readers. Similarly, as they look at a book, website, article, or essay, they may also struggle to know how to jump in, where to enter the conversation, and, even if they do read, what to do with that information once they have consumed it.

Working with highly motivated students in an honors course is both a blessing and a curse. On the one hand, they are eager to learn and willing to take risks. On the other hand, they want clearly defined paths for that learning and risks that ultimately don't push them so far out of their comfort zone that they freeze. This past year, when organizing his freshman seminar as a writing-intensive course focused on digital identity, Troy provided students with a number of "pathways" that they could explore, in small groups and as inquiry-driven projects. While he knew that this would be a bit of a pedagogical challenge, it turned out to be even more complicated than he had predicted. With the first pathway that all students were asked to complete, the digital identity narrative discussed in Chapter 1, students were struggling to discover exactly the ways in which they wanted to share their work.

Despite the opportunities for choice in terms of topics as well as the digital writing formats in which they could share their work, students were somewhat frustrated because they could not find clear outlines, checklists, or rubrics. Then, as the weeks wore on, and even when provided with guiding questions and opportunities for further exploration—as well as ideas for creating particular multimodal projects—students still struggled with figuring out exactly what they wanted to accomplish as a group. Conversations about infinite possibilities quickly evolved into stress and confusion as students struggled: Where can we find additional academic resources? Who can we interview? What kind of media project should we create? Even for a room full of eager honors students, the traditional pressures of grades, checklists, and rubrics pushed them back into traditional roles.

Troy learned from this first, very open-ended pathway that he had to provide a bit more structure for students as they progressed through their next two pathways with their groups. And, as we will discuss later in the chapter, the "pathway planners" and "project proposal" assignments that he created, while not a perfect

---

BOX 2.2: Teachers Can Help Students Become Better Writers

It is in our nature to set goals for our students and to help them reach the expectations we have designed. Still, NCTE states in *Professional Knowledge* that, "[i]n order to provide high-quality writing opportunities for all students, teachers need to understand . . . how to ensure that every student has the tools and supports necessary to be as independent as possible" (2016). Helping students identify their own needs—and teaching them how to address those needs—is equally as important as any content we are expected to cover.

solution, did help students focus on the tasks at hand. As Troy was reminded during the process of teaching his seminar, giving students enough structure to set their goals—without being overly prescriptive—is the key to good teaching and at the core of creating confident writers.

Again, we invite you to join us in collegial conversation about approaches to writing, this time focused on setting goals. When teaching writing, we consider these questions related to goal setting:

- Through the daily routines we've established and the assignments we've created, do we invite our students to be agents in their own learning?
- By modeling our personal reading and writing goals, do we share the kinds of reading and writing goals we want students to create?
- Through the conversations we have about writing, do we help students move from initial brainstorming to meaningful project planning?
- Over the course of a trimester or semester, do we capitalize on the "fresh start effect" by seeking naturally occurring moments for writers to set goals and fueling their motivation?

Harnessing the Fresh Start Effect

Beginnings are important. So important, in fact, that social scientists call these memorable moments "temporal landmarks" or, in other words, natural checkpoints where people pause, reflect, and assess personal goals. Dubbed the "fresh start effect" in a study by Hengchen Dai, Katherine Milkman, and Jason Riis, "temporal landmarks interrupt attention to day-to-day minutiae, causing people to take a big picture view of their lives and thus focus on achieving their goals" (2014, p. 2577). The fresh start effect is useful for students and teachers alike because, as Daniel Pink notes, "days that represent 'firsts' switch on people's motivation" (2018, p. 94) and allow students to share a set of realistic goals from a naturally occurring reflective stance. Whether consciously or unconsciously, writers, too, take advantage of temporal landmarks to create goals for themselves and use timelines to measure how well they are meeting those goals.

Though we may not consider it often, there are many beginnings purposefully sprinkled within a daily workshop model, over the course of a week, and certainly within the context of a larger unit. Beyond the first days of a course, we can intentionally plan temporal landmarks—or the beginning of new routines—that create dedicated spaces for building literacy habits.

Of the more common temporal landmarks that we are happy to see in classrooms across the country, dedicated classroom time for independent reading is crucial. There are mountains of research, more than we can cite here, supporting the idea that sustained, in-class, independent reading time increases the likelihood of students building a reading identity (for the most complete, contemporary list we could find, see Beers & Probst, 2017). Many professional writers are voracious readers. Stephen King is very blunt on the subject: "If you don't have time to read, you don't have time (or the tools) to write. Simple as that" (2010, p. 142).

For Hannah Peless, a twelfth-grade student and a voracious reader, reading is instrumental in her growth as a writer. She understands the reading/writing connection well and how it transfers into her writing:

> *I draw skills from my favorite authors, observing how carefully they crafted sentences so they would stick with you. I read all sorts of things when I was younger, from* Magic Tree House *to* The Hobbit. *With every book I picked up, I absorbed a little bit of that author's writing soul.*

A less common, though no less important, temporal landmark that we would like to see in classrooms across the country is dedicated classroom time for independent creative writing. Though the research here is not as robust as it is for independent reading, Andy supports the idea that sustained, in-class, independent creative writing increases the likelihood of building a writing identity for students.

After a few weeks of experiencing independent creative writing in his classes, which include invitations to write, encouragement to share, and a celebration of words, Andy's students begin a process of transforming their attitudes toward writing. He finds that dedicated creative writing time is engaging for students and increases their motivation to write as they develop a sense of community in his classroom.

For Taylor Williams, a twelfth-grade student and an emerging poet, independent creative writing reignited a love for writing that was almost extinguished. She attributes dedicated time to write creatively as an experience that built her writing confidence. "As a writer," she says, "I find myself now wanting to share my poems and other work because I am very proud of them. I found my passion for writing again and found a new one for poetry."

In literacy curriculum saturated with academic-style prose, Anne Lamott makes a case for the inclusion of independent creative writing in her classic work,

---

BOX 2.3: Writing and Reading Are Related

Providing students with time to read and write may feel as if we are "taking away" from a crowded curriculum when, instead, they are essential instructional practices. Two segments of NCTE's *Professional Knowledge* are pertinent here.

First, with the principle that reading and writing are related, we see that "[i]n order to provide high-quality writing opportunities for all students, teachers need to understand . . . one way teachers help students become better writers is to make sure they have lots of extended time to read, in school and out."

Second, with the principle that writing grows out of many purposes, NCTE contends that "[i]n order to provide high-quality writing opportunities for all students, teachers need to understand . . . ways people use writing for personal growth, expression, and reflection, and how to encourage and develop this kind of writing" (2016).

Bird by Bird (1995). Regarding creative writing, she says, "you get your intuition back when you make space for it, when you stop the chattering of the rational mind." She asserts that "rationality squeezes out much that is rich and juicy and fascinating" (p. 112). There is, indeed, a place for many genres of writing in the classroom, including academic writing, but we should create moments for students to explore creatively as well.

We are convinced that the three structures critical for any reading and writing workshop are (at the risk of oversimplifying): reading, writing, and sharing. Each structure is interdependent and symbiotic. Reading is a natural part of a writing process and vice versa. Sharing our literate lives makes them real. You cannot have any one of these three without the others. By making room in the day for all three, we set the course for habits that lead to reading and writing goals for our students.

Daily Routines for Reading, Writing, and Sharing

We consider these structures essential for creating confident writers because we know that some of our students are able to carve out time in the day for these practices in their lives outside of school, but many cannot or do not. Writers who know they will have time in their class every day to read, write, and share build literacy habits and gain momentum as confident writers. Of course, providing reading time in Troy's college class, which meets for only 2.5 hours per week and 45 contact hours in a semester, is difficult; still, there are days when he will invite students to read a text in class before discussing it with peers, or to take some time to write. Even with precious little time, he makes space for it, showing students that he values reading and writing enough to devote some of their limited time to the practice.

For Andy, in a high school classroom, things are also busy, yet he still has the opportunity to help students build these habits. The interplay between reading and writing is so inclusive that dedicating time for creative writing, which is detailed in Activity 1.1 in Chapter 1, is just as important as class time for dedicated independent reading. There are days that are dedicated for writing and those that are for reading, though there is still flexibility in that schedule depending on the students' needs, the curriculum, and all the other variables of school schedules. Building on the ideas presented in Chapter 1 and Figure 1.1, in particular, a closer look at Andy's daily and weekly schedule provides insight on how he dedicates space for reading and writing in a rotating schedule throughout the week (see Table 2.1).

In short, the structure of the workshop on any given day is flexible; nonetheless, the consistency of the workshop approach, over time, allows students to

TABLE 2.1: Sample of a Weekly Schedule Designed for Flexible Structure

	Monday	**Tuesday**	**Wednesday**	**Thursday**	**Friday**
Opening	Daily poem	Daily poem	Daily poem	Daily poem	Daily poem
Segment 1	Independent reading	Creative writing	Independent reading	Creative writing	Independent reading
Segment 2	Mini-lesson	Student sharing	Mini-lesson	Student sharing	Mini-lesson
Segment 3	Workshop time	Mini-lesson	Workshop time	Mini-lesson	Workshop time
Closing	Student sharing	Workshop time	Student sharing	Workshop time	Student sharing

BOX 2.4: Writing Is a Process

To live in the mantra that "writing is a process," we agree with NCTE's point in the *Professional Knowledge* that "[i]n order to provide high-quality writing opportunities for all students, teachers need to understand . . . how to design time and possibly staged intervals of work for students to do their best on a given assignment." If we provide the structure, and still allow for some flexibility, our students will become comfortable and confident as they work on their writing, day in and day out.

set goals and plan for substantive reading and writing activity. They can set goals because they know they will have the time, space, and support to pursue—and attain—them.

Inviting students to create self-selected goals grounds them in their own language. They become active participants in their own learning as they create personal accountability targets. These targets, moreover, are the ones they are aiming for and, though they may not hit all of them, by writing them down they are acknowledging personal areas of growth they are interested in achieving. For our students, writing goals typically fall into the categories we refer to as 1) developing a fascination, 2) aiming for daily improvement, 3) striving for emotional or spiritual ideals that relate to being literate, and 4) adopting a growth mindset. Each serves a different purpose for goal setting and each evokes questions that give insight into our students.

These broad categories of questions, which help both Andy and Troy frame what they talk about—and ask of—students, come in four themes. We will not explicitly ask each of these questions of any particular student on any given day; still, keeping these bigger ideas in mind helps us stay focused when talking with students about their own goals (see Table 2.2).

Our goal, of course, is to create the conditions necessary to help students become as independent as possible. By acknowledging their own goals, they are able to visualize what they hope to achieve. Goal-setting opportunities, like these, take advantage of the fresh start effect and meet students right where they are in the beginning stages of a course. In these moments, it is natural for students to consider where they have been, where they are now, and where they would like to be as writers. Each is a consideration on the pathway toward independence.

TABLE 2.2: Guiding Questions for Setting Goals with Reading and Writing

	In the Moment	Projecting to the Future
Developing a Fascination	What questions are most intriguing to you? What are the things you are curious about?	By the end of the unit/trimester (semester), what topics will you hope to have explored during our time together?
Aiming for Daily Improvement	How do you carve out time each day for reading and writing both inside and outside of school? What are your reading and writing hurdles and how do you plan to overcome them?	What do you hope you will be able to say about your daily reading and writing habits?
Striving for Emotional or Spiritual Ideals that Relate to Being Literate	How do your literacy goals match your broader goals for school? What does it mean to be literate in your personal life?	What value do reading and writing bring to your life outside of school?
Adopting a Growth Mindset	What does it mean to be open and flexible when it comes to new learning or new experiences? How might these ideas help you disrupt beliefs that your abilities are fixed and to find that you can continue to grow as a reader and writer?	Which habits of mind do you hope to practice in your own life? How do you plan to be more persistent when writing challenges emerge?

When writers surround themselves with beautiful words, probing thoughts, and emerging ideas, it is hard not to want to be a part of it. Reading and writing goals are habits of mind that invite openness. Writers who read are often eager to write themselves, because the more joy they find in books the sooner they think to themselves, *I can write like that!* Which, of course, they can. Helping them set goals, then, becomes a key part of the invitations and encouragement that we offer them on their path to becoming confident writers. These daily structures and conversations are but a few ways we invite students to connect with their writing goals.

BOX 2.5: Teachers Can Help Students Become Better Writers

Knowing that writing is not just a "gift" bestowed upon certain people, and that it can be taught in a systematic manner, NCTE's *Professional Knowledge* reminds us that "[i]n order to provide high-quality writing opportunities for all students, teachers need to understand . . . how to ensure that every student has the tools and supports necessary to be as independent as possible." In doing so, we are helping them move through the four connected practices described in Table 2.2.

In our classrooms, goal setting plays a role and the fresh start effect accompanies us along the way.

Writing Activities that Help Students Set Goals

With the activities described in the next section, we show how our second principle of invitation comes through the process of setting goals and works as a way to take advantage of the fresh start effect, ensuring that student agency is a part of their literacy curriculum. For Andy, this begins by asking students to document their own literacy journeys.

ACTIVITY 2.1:

Living Your Literacy Journey

Having built off of the great examples provided by Nancie Atwell (1998, 2014) and Penny Kittle (2008), Andy has developed a series of questions, based on reading and writing surveys that he has encountered over the years, built around four topics/themes. Students write about each of these four ideas in a series of ten-minute quick writes, all four occurring during one class period. He invites them to consider the following:

- **Literacy Experiences:** Where have I been? What are my literacy roots? What are my literacy branches?
  — What does your current reading/writing life look like?
  — What are the ways in which you read/write on your own? How does this compare with reading/writing in school?
  — How would you describe your relationship with reading/writing? Are you currently "in a relationship"? "seeking a relationship"? "on again, off again"? or "not interested"? Share your reasoning.
  — What keeps your relationship with reading alive? What are you looking for in a reading relationship? What pushes you away from reading?

- **Challenges and Sparks – Reading:** Who am I as a reader?
  — What are the challenges, both small and significant, that have affected your abilities and confidence as a reader?
  — What have been your challenges with reading?
  — What topics, genres, and authors excite you?
  — What are your passions, interests, and deeply held beliefs about how you learn best as a reader?
  — Recall and reflect on your reading sparks: What pulls you into reading?
  — How might what you read impact how/what you write?

- **Challenges and Sparks – Writing**: Who am I as a writer?
  — What are the challenges, both small and significant, that have affected your abilities and confidence as a writer?
  — What have been your challenges with writing?
  — What topics, genres, and authors excite you?
  — What are your passions, interests, and deeply held beliefs about how you learn best as a writer?
  — Recall and reflect on your writing sparks: What pulls you into writing?
  — How might what you write impact how/what you read?

- **Literacy Goals:** Where do I want to be?
  — What are three to four reading and writing goals you have for the trimester?

- How many books do you plan on reading?
- Are you interested in writing for real audiences?
- Have you considered a form of publication, whether it be small or significant?

— What habits of mind might you need to accomplish these goals?

Once students finish their draft, Andy introduces them to Edublogs, a free blogging platform available for teachers and students (link on the authors' website), models how to set up a blog, and shows them a few key features to get them started (examples of student blogs are available at this chapter's page on the authors' website). After the mini-lesson, they have become a bit distanced from their quick writes, which gives them the space they need to write their first post—their literacy journey with reading and writing goals written for the trimester.

It is one thing to write your own goals, but group accountability can be a meaningful incentive to strive for the goals that students create. To make the blogs a bit more authentic, Andy links all the blogs to his classroom web page; the next day, students respond to one another's journey and Andy encourages them to reach their chosen goals. To do so, he responds to every student's literacy journey with positivity, empathy, and encouragement.

There is much to be learned about the literate lives of students when they share their journeys. In order to gain a better perspective and insight, let's pause and zoom in on one student, Esme Bailey. As a twelfth-grade student who has taken honors courses throughout high school and chose to take a college prep course, AP Literature and Composition, Esme's writing and reading experience seem to follow a trend that is all too predictable. While she had an interest in reading and writing in her earlier years, by high school that passion was dampened by curricular goals and grades. In the next section, we explore her "Literacy Journey," originally published on her blog (Bailey, 2018).

Esme was raised in a literacy-rich environment, and she was fortunate to have fond memories of reading to herself, as well as to and with her parents, friends, and teachers. Often finding time to write at home, she also reminisces on her love of writing by telling how, in the second grade, she discovered that "art class was no longer the right exit for this creativity that was swelling inside of [her] ready to explode." She readily admits that she loved English when she was growing up.

BOX 2.6: Esme's Literacy Journey

My E.L.A. Journey: From Beginning to Other Beginnings
Esme Bailey

As a young child, my parents always urged me to read. In the beginning, titles such as *What Was I Scared Of?* by Dr. Seuss and Little Golden Books such as *The Little Red Hen* sparked a fire that would engulf me as I grew older. As I started my long journey in the local public school system, my teachers seemed to be amazed at my reading ability.

In the third grade, I read *Oliver Twist* by Charles Dickens and this really turned my head. I was moved by this older language that spoke to me in a way other books hadn't. This led me to read other famous titles, such as *Pride and Prejudice*, *Anne of Green Gables*, and *Dracula* by the time I was in the sixth grade. After finding my love for reading, I expected to always feel the need to read.

To my dismay, my desire to read died off in the seventh grade. That year, I was given books that I was forced to read for a grade in my English class. Due to my strong feelings when it came to my grades and the necessity of having them be perfect, reading was no longer a treasured time; but rather an activity that I had to do no matter if I liked the book or not. Of course, as it does in the public education systems of America, the tradition of putting the metaphorical gun to my head to read some atrocious book carried on through the rest of my educational journey. Now don't get me wrong, I'm still a reader at heart and I know that I always will be, but sometimes it doesn't have the spark that I crave from so long ago.

Stating strongly that I am a writer is a bit more difficult than stating that I'm a reader. I learned to write while I was in the second grade, roughly. I suppose that was the year that art class was no longer the right exit for this creativity that was swelling inside of me ready to explode. I suppose that is why most people write, though; to let their creativity flow through their own words in their own time. Now, I used to think writing was a skill, but I now know that writing is something that anyone and everyone can do. I say this with confidence because all writing takes is time and the ability to express oneself through words.

When it comes to writing well, I would say the term 'writing well' a subjective. I believe that writing well is something more personal than a basic standard to meet. My own personal writing is something I take pride in because of my growth over the years, which I can say is from more life experience. As I write, I try to block my thoughts from my mind so they flow efficiently onto whatever form of writing I'm working on.

> While reading and writing are my two biggest hobbies at the moment, I know that there is and always will be room for improvement. Right now, my first goal is to once again fall head-over-heels in love with reading again. I think a great second goal is to go back to my roots and read more classic novels. My third goal is to get myself out of this sticky situation I find myself in with not evolving my reading skills. I yearn to read more advanced books and not have to stop every two paragraphs in order to look the meaning of words up. I want to read classics confidently and understand what's going on . . . at least for most of the time.

Yet she cites middle school as the time when her love for English was spoiled. It was specifically in the seventh grade, where she "was given books that [she] was forced to read [and write about] . . . in [her] English class," and this continued throughout middle school. Once curricula and grades took priority over a love for literacy, Esme began to view reading and writing "no longer as a treasured time, but rather an activity that [she] had to do no matter if [she] liked the book or not."

Esme insists that she is "still a reader [and writer] at heart" but acknowledges that "it doesn't have the spark that [she craves] from so long ago." Esme, unfortunately, is not alone. The troubling matter is that she is an honors student with college set firmly in her mind, and yet she has felt the pressures seeking personal achievement. No longer did school seem like a place where Esme—or thousands upon thousands of other students—could grow, explore, play, and learn. Instead, it was about marching through books, assignments, essays, and tests.

Looking at it from another perspective, prolific public speaker and creativity expert Sir Ken Robinson agrees and asserts that the problem is systemic. He understands that "one of the roles of education is to awaken and develop [the] powers of creativity. Instead, what we have is a culture of standardization" (Robinson, 2013). Robinson would say that experiences like Esme's are pervasive. He argues that we should not be surprised by this because students have become habituated to school or, in a dire turn of phrase, "they have become educated." In other words, a standardized education system stifles creativity and, therefore, minimizes the importance of the creative work of writing. As teachers of writing, we know that there is, however, hope for those willing to rise above the standards.

BOX 2.7: Responsibility and Engagement

By writing her literacy journey, Esme took on the responsibility of reflecting on her experiences, challenges, sparks, and goals to, as the *Framework* suggests, "recognize [her] own role in learning." Additionally, the process engaged her in the search to "find meanings new to [her] or build on existing meanings as a result of new connections." Further, the experience invited Esme to engage in critical thinking that then allowed her to "extend and synthesize [her] thinking." Our students need invitations like these built into our busy days, or else it is very likely that they will not take time to engage in this kind of reflection on their own.

Esme is, indeed, a student who knows herself as a learner. In a reflective moment of her "Literacy Journey," Esme shared "that is why most people write, though; to let their creativity flow through their own words in their own time." Moreover, in her statement we recognize that it was in those moments when her teachers relinquished control to choose a flexible and responsive pedagogy that she was empowered as a reader, writer, and thinker.

Through this process, students are able to articulate many key aspects of their literate lives, inviting us, as teachers, to gain a glimpse into what they value and where they struggle.

Esme's "Literacy Journey" reminds us that students who are empowered have a choice and a voice when it comes to their learning. It makes sense because, as learners, empowerment is a place each of us longs to be. And, while neither of us have perfected this yet, we do have some ideas for how to enable empowering goal-setting practices in our writing classrooms. Asking students to share their experiences, challenges, sparks, and goals is one way to move in this direction. Another way is to help them imagine their literate lives in the future.

ACTIVITY 2.2:
A Letter to Future Me

After considering the goals they generated in their "Literacy Journey," students use the website FutureMe (the link is available at this chapter's page on the authors' website) to send a reminder of their goals to themselves at, of course, a future date. In their letter, students write about what they plan to accomplish over the course of the trimester. Viewing this writing experience as a "preflection," Andy reminds his students that they should "recognize their own role in learning" (Falk, p. 5), and this letter serves as a unique opportunity to do so. As they write, he encourages them to be persistent, to be kind to themselves, and to think about their own literacy strengths and weaknesses (Falk, 1995).

Before students send their letter to the future, Andy selects a date that matches the Monday of the last week of the trimester. At the end of the trimester they see if they met their reading and writing goals, share what went well and areas they still need to work on. In this way, students use the trimester as a timeline to gauge how well they are meeting their goals. Though Andy is intentional in telling students he does not expect, nor even want, to have access to the "Future Me" letters, a few students are eager to share what they have written.

For instance, we share another part of Esme's journey. Her "Future Me" letter was particularly insightful regarding her reading and writing goals:

"Dear Future Me,
I hope this past trimester has been one for the books, because right now you need something memorable like that. As you know, English classes have been so monochromatic for as long as you can remember, so again, hopefully this class was a rainbow. A few things that have been on my mind lately (as in the-past-decade lately) is how reading has fallen off of my to-do list. Of course reading has been something that has been similar to a comfort object for you, but lately it's been covered in dirt and crumbs and blah. Anywho, one of your goals this past trimester was to find that spark again. If that didn't happen, that's okay because we can try again. Remember that falling in love isn't a thing that typically happens after the first date.

Other than reading, I seriously hope that you found something/ someone who you can really talk to because, again, you need some of that right now. I know that you sometimes write for pleasure, but maybe you found a way to write for others, as well as yourself? Regardless, I just really hope that all is well in every way, shape, and form. Also that you're taking care of yourself, and that you get everything in order to fill out those college applications!! Good luck with everything that's about to come for you girl.

With love,

You but younger"

Tucked within Esme's letter to herself is a common thread many students have for classes they are entering: hope. Our students come into our classrooms with the experiences of previous English classes nestled inside their minds. These experiences cover a vast range of teachers, teaching styles, and emotions. The "Future Me" letter is a moment for students to sit down with themselves and consider their personal literacy goals for class.

As with many goal-setting exercises in life, students often perceive the letter to "Future Me" as a bit awkward, or even forgettable, during the moments in which they write it. For Andy, that's an acceptable feeling, and he invites students to acknowledge and live into that feeling. As a moment in which they are identifying and considering their goals, this becomes a chance for them to think carefully about what they want to do, as readers and writers, in the weeks ahead.

In the broader goal of creating confident writers, the "Future Me" letter fits into a series of pieces. As mentioned earlier in this chapter, the "Literacy Journey" is the first piece of this puzzle, followed by students' current assessment of themselves as readers and writers. This "Future Me" message will appear in their inbox twelve weeks hence, on the Monday of the exam week. This letter, which they have invariably forgotten about, suddenly appears in their inbox as they prepare to take their reflective final exam (which will be described in more detail in Chapter 6). Like most students, Esme smiled as she opened her "Future Me" letter and began chatting with her friends. While she did not meet every goal, she was pleased with the many goals that she did meet.

As their confidence with low-stakes literacy habits grow, students find their confidence growing for higher-stakes academic writing as well. These low-stakes opportunities, which rarely count for a grade and are, most

---

BOX 2.8: Responsibility and Persistence

By writing her letter to a "future me," students like Esme demonstrate two additional habits of mind, as outlined in the *Framework*. They take on the responsibility of setting personal (and often privvate) literacy goals to "recognize [her] own role in learning." Moreover, she created a sense of persistence to "follow through, over time, to complete tasks, processes, or projects." As noted throughout the first two chapters, we as teachers of writing must build these invitations into our workshop routines, as it is unlikely that most students would choose to engage in deep, sustained reflection without a few nudges along the way.

---

often, a chance for our writers to try a new approach or reflect on their work, are crucial. When it comes to academic writing, it is at times tempting to spend little time prewriting or brainstorming for a larger manuscript. The perceived pressure of time to write often causes students to zoom by the critical process of situating themselves with intention before embarking on a complex writing opportunity. These low-stakes literacy practices become a routine, a comfortable component of students' writing process.

ACTIVITY 2.3:
Intentional Planning with Project Proposals

As writers ourselves, we agree that a process of writing need not follow a linear pattern beginning with prewriting and ending in a final draft. Yet we recognize that forethought is a requirement for creating writing goals and gaining the confidence needed to follow through. Having both been in the professional world of English teachers—and in talking with our family and friends about their own professional worlds, too—both Andy and Troy recognize that writing often begins with a proposal.

For instance, a majority of invitations to present at a conference or to publish an article, book, or other monograph all begin with submitting proposals. For the writer, the act of creating a proposal helps focus the work, providing the writer direction. For the stakeholders, the submission of a proposal indicates personal investment. For both, proposals stage the writer's purpose and intent. This begs the following questions for student writers: what is *their* purpose? what is *their* intent? and, perhaps most important, *so what?*

Proposals generate a writer's agency. There is power in owning your own learning as a sense of engagement emerges in the process. Not meant to be painstakingly detailed, the proposal sets the stage for what's ahead. It grounds writers in their personal investment in the piece. Typical outlining processes that students might be accustomed to are too topical, thus generating a list of basic ideas and failing to get the author (or authors) fully invested in the early stages of writing the piece. Similarly, brainstorming or mind mapping don't always hit the target of investment.

In Chapter 4, Responding to Reading, we will see another example of how Andy's students outline a project proposal for a critical theory paper. For the moment, let's examine a proposal form that Troy created. Even high-achieving students struggle to figure out exactly what they could or should be doing when tackling an open-ended project. Hindsight being what it is, Troy quickly realized after the Digital ID project that students needed at least some concrete steps and deadlines for their subsequent learning pathways.

The project proposal document helps students coordinate their efforts as a group, focused on their inquiry question and the ultimate project that they wanted to create (a link to the Google Doc template for the project proposal can be found on the authors' website page for Chapter 2). Using the MAPS heuristic that he outlined in *Crafting Digital Writing* (2013), Troy asks students to consider a number of points in the initial proposal for their multimedia projects. First, students must examine the mode or genre of the writing, considering the purposes that this type of writing typically aims to accomplish. Then, they must choose the media types that will exist in piece of writing. For traditional essays, words are formed into sentences, sentences into paragraphs, and then into full manuscripts. With digital writing—whether a word-processed essay, a blog post, or other form of multimedia—we can also have students explore options for including images, video, charts, maps or other elements. Next, we invite students to consider audiences (beyond the teacher) as well as purposes (beyond earning a grade), helping them envision possibilities for sharing their writing outside the classroom. Lastly, MAPS encourages students to think about their own abilities as writers (what they know and are able to do, as well as what they want to learn) and to consider deadlines, assignment expectations, and other contextual factors. In the Project Proposal document, the MAPS heuristic is used explicitly, as shown in Table 2.3. Again, a link to the Project Proposal template is available on the authors' website.

Students from one of Troy's recent writing intensive courses, Lori Cook and Julia Amting (who was introduced in Chapter 1), worked with their part-

TABLE 2.3: Project Proposal Elements and Questions

Project Element	Description of Element	Questions to Consider in the Proposal
Mode	The genre or style of the writing	• What are the characteristics of the genre of a [_____]? • What are the types of structures that writers use? • What counts as evidence in this community?
Media	Text, images, video, charts, maps or other multimedia elements	• What do you need to learn about using audio, video, images, maps, hyperlinks, or other digital writing tools? • How does this media enhance your overall argument?
Audience	The intended and incidental audiences for which the writing is designed	• Move beyond a "general audience" and describe who, specifically, you are writing for, considering the demographics (age, regional location, income level, etc.) and psychographics (values, interests, concerns, affiliations, etc.). • What do they believe? • What counts as evidence for this audience?
Purpose	The stance that the writer(s) take(s), as indicated by the tone of the writing, the use of evidence, and other rhetorical choices	• Choose an active verb. What are you trying to do with your writing? • Write more about this verb and how your purpose is going to guide your work on this project.
Situation	The context for both the writer(s) and the writing task itself	• What do you know about this genre? This topic? • What will you have to learn about the technology that you plan to use? • What else do you need help with as you move toward a final project?

ners to develop a multimedia project about "The History and Legends of CMU," which we will explore as a fully formed project in Chapter 3. For the moment, it is important to understand how the project proposal helped Lori and Julia imagine possibilities with their group. They began by looking at the broad category of travel writing; then they chose a tool, Story Maps JS, created by the Knight Lab for journalism at Northwestern University (the link is available at the authors' website), which would allow them to make an interactive map of CMU's campus.

Because they had limited experience composing multimedia texts, Lori and Julia's group noted in their proposal that they "need[ed] to become familiar with several types of media." Moreover, "having never used a tool like it, it is going to take some time to figure out how it works and all of the features that it has, specifically regarding images and maps." The group also realized that their audience would "consist of a variety of ages and demographics, but united under the common interest of CMU and its history."

Beyond the technical aspects of using Story Maps JS, the group's proposal noted that "our group will need to work on making sense of the multiple interpretations of the stories we hear." In this sense, the project proposal helped them determine what they wanted to accomplish, and then gave Troy some insights on how to help coach them in the weeks to come.

Invitations to write, reflect, and share literacy goals create opportunities for students to invest in themselves as learners. When teachers invite students to see themselves as active participants in their learning, they build the confidence needed to move toward independence. As teacher-

---

BOX 2.9: Responsibility and Persistence

By using the MAPS heuristic, Lori and Julia paused to "recognize their own role in learning" as they worked in a group to "grapple with challenging ideas, texts, processes, or projects," as described in the *Framework*. Discovering the precise angle that they wanted to pursue for their Story Map was a challenge, and the experience invited Lori and Julia's group to consider their audience, purpose, and intent. All of this demonstrates how they were developing flexible writing processes to "generate ideas and texts using a variety of processes and situate those ideas within different academic disciplines and contexts."

writers, we understand the role that goal setting plays in our professional lives. We also understand our own struggles with the agency we experience when our personal goals don't seem to mesh with those placed on us. Furthermore, we acknowledge that the goals, standards, missions, and visions of schools and universities are important to the quality of the education students receive. Yet, within those larger institutional goals, we are able to carve out some room to honor the personal literacy goals of our students, and we are sure to find a balance that suits everyone's needs.

Conclusion

When we consider the ways in which we invite our student writers to identify, attain, and revise their own goals, we move into some uncomfortable spaces. It is, without a doubt, challenging for us as teachers to move from whole-class instruction to individualized learning. Moreover, finding ways to create spaces for student-centered goals within the boundaries of curriculum, standardized testing, and district and university missions can, at times, seem challenging. Yet it is within these challenging spaces and times that we must consider how we create writing goals, for what purpose, and for whom. Consider the following questions:

- How might you model, demonstrate, or share your own reading and writing goals with your students?
- In what ways could you help students set their own reading and writing goals? How might honoring their goals help create confident readers and writers?
- While we are all expected to teach certain curriculum, texts, and skills, with which of these do you have some flexibility that, in turn, you might work with your students to set their own goals?
- With digital writing, what additional goals might students establish for themselves in order to take advantage of spaces like their own blogs, sharing their ideas with a wider audience?

ENCOURAGE

CHAPTER 3

Exploring Mentor Texts

"I grew as a writer by using mentor texts and, through utilizing them, was able to produce some of my best work yet."

—Taylor Idema, MPHS

Exploring Mentor Texts Creates Confident Writers by . . .

- Showing writers models that they can emulate, from a few words to entire essays;
- Inspiring them to make choices about tone and style, taking a risk with their writer's voice;
- Sparking their curiosity about new authors, genres, and means of publication;
- Bringing the eye of the writer to their perspective as readers, looking for inspiration in fiction, nonfiction, and multimedia.

Fear of the unknown is a stumbling block for many writers, and, at the same time, it is the exploration of the unknown world that is exciting. Few of us are brave enough to blaze a trail into the unknown without leaning on the guidance and encouragement of a mentor—be it person or text. Mentors and mentor texts serve as light in the darkness of the unknown world.

We admire the work of Allison Marchetti and Rebekah O'Dell, who define mentor texts as "model pieces of writing—or excerpts of writing—by established authors that can inspire students and teach them how to write" (2015, p. 3). To extend this idea, Katherine Bomer suggests that we "pay attention to what we see, hear, and feel as we read . . . closely. We can notice for ourselves what . . . stir[s] up in the minds and hearts of readers and then make that seeing explicit . . . in our own writing" (2016, p. 1).

When writers are encouraged to seek the guidance of mentor texts with an open mind, they can learn what good writing looks like, what it sounds like, and what it feels like. They can apply those moves in their own writing. This is challenging work, however, for many of our students who have learned that writing for school boils down to five-paragraph structures, scripted templates, and stifling rubrics. In his high school classroom, Andy pushes his students to move past the confines of writing for school, in the traditional sense, and encourages them to trust models they find compelling.

One of his students, Andrea, echoes what lies in the heart of many student writers venturing beyond the five-paragraph formula. She admits that "the very notion of writing essays any other way was quite literally a huge leap of faith for me." We, as teachers, can be mentors for students like Andrea, who need help learning to trust a process of writing instead of relying on formulas. Mentor texts move student writers beyond the five-paragraph essay; they give a glimpse of what writing looks like in the real world; and they model rhetorical moves that increase a reader's investment in a text.

As a mentor in your own classroom, inviting, encouraging, and celebrating writing are all critical to build the confidence within your students to write. In the first two chapters we narrowed our focus on writing invitations in the spaces we create and how those spaces lead to student writing goals. We pivot here, and for the next two chapters focus on moments within texts—as well as the moments

---

BOX 3.2: Writing and Reading Are Related

Looking at mentor texts, as Stephen King's quote in Chapter 2 reminds us, is essential for writers if they want to become better at their craft. NCTE concurs in *Professional Knowledge*, noting that "[i]n order to provide high-quality writing opportunities for all students, teachers need to understand . . . writers read for the purposes of writing—with an eye toward not just what the text says but also how it is put together." Every day, from small moments to full lessons, it is worth our while as teachers to talk with students about the ways in which texts are constructed so they can gain a deeper appreciation for other writers and use similar techniques in their own writing.

they share with one another—each of which encourage students to write in spite of the fear of the unknown. We encourage you to be a writing mentor with your students, lifting up mentor texts as lights in the dark to overcome their writing fears.

We encourage you to join us in collegial conversation about approaches to writing, this time focused on exploring mentor texts. When teaching writing, we consider these questions:

- Through the assignments we create, do we encourage our students to broaden their definition of a text to include digital, multimodal, and visual texts?
- Through mini-lessons that reveal how we read texts as writers, do we model our own processes of deconstructing mentor texts to encourage students to experiment and play with writing?
- By comparing professional mentor texts to peer mentor texts, do we move students from emulating a mentor text to making intentional rhetorical decisions for their own writing?
- Over the course of a trimester or semester, do we provide opportunities for students to share their writing with authentic audiences?

Mentors and Mentor Texts Inspire Fearless Writing

Mentors inspire. They demonstrate a way of being that resonates with others. Oftentimes, mentors veer from the expected pathway to reveal new ways of envisioning the world.

Consider for a moment the real-life mentors you have claimed as your own. Most likely they attracted your attention by qualities you admire, and you were interested in weaving those qualities into your own life. Mentor texts are meant to do the same; they capture the ordinary in unexpected and interesting ways. They offer glimpses of what can be possible if we, as writers, think divergently and stay open to varied ways of writing in the world.

Mentor texts teach. When we attune our writer's eye to their structure, tone, craft, voice, and movements, we gain confidence to break free from our default writing styles, incorporating nuanced movements in our thinking.

Marchetti and O'Dell know the power that mentor texts hold to help students not only by seeing writing beyond the walls of the classroom but also in the quiet nudges of encouragement they offer writers. In their work, *Writing with Mentors* (2015), they assert that:

" . . . mentor texts enable student writers to become connected to the dynamic world of professional writers. Mentor texts enable independence as, over time, students are able to find and use the inspiration and craft elements found in the sentences and pages of their favorite writers." (p. 3)

It is a writer's independence we seek to help in order to build the confidence students need to trust themselves and move their conversations from the classroom to the real world. We are interested in helping students realize that there is an audience for their ideas and that their voice is needed in the world. When students look closely at texts as mentors, they begin to rub elbows with professional writers as they enter into conversations happening all around them. For both of us, mentor texts help students see possibilities well beyond the five-paragraph essay; they help students like Andrea see how their writing could move beyond traditional structures. As we will continue to explore in this chapter and the rest of the book, using mentor texts to explore various genres, audiences, purposes, and even different media than we typically see in academic writing means that students are exposed to intellectually rigorous ideas in alternative formats.

Encouraging Exploration with Digital Literacies

As children, our students were encouraged to connect via video chats with their aunts, uncles, friends, and grandparents who may live across the country. As children, our students grew up on the other side of smartphone camera lenses as loved ones snapped—and shared on social media—untold numbers of pictures and videos documenting their lives. As our young people continued to grow up in this digital world, some found their way, through friends, to social media platforms like Snapchat, Instagram, and Twitter. There are many reasons why our students are drawn to connect socially through digital means. At the heart is the innate desire to explore new territories, try on different voices, and share with authentic audiences.

This is important for a number of reasons, not the least of which is that students—who are accustomed to social media posts, images, vlogs, and other methods of short-form writing—can begin to see the ways in which technology can be used to support longer, more substantive compositions. Moreover, in reading (as well as viewing and listening to) many voices from diverse authors (including photographers, filmmakers, podcasters, and other multimedia producers),

---

BOX 3.3: Writing Is Embedded in Complex Social Relationships and Their Appropriate Languages

---

Over the past forty years, NCTE has progressively adopted more and more position statements and resolutions about the role of media in our students' lives. From the *Professional Knowledge* statement, they reiterate this commitment by arguing that "[i]n order to provide high-quality writing opportunities for all students, teachers need to understand . . . the ways digital environments have added new modalities while constantly creating new publics, audiences, purposes, and invitations to compose." Both Andy and Troy are deeply committed to the goal of engaging students in digital writing, as we will share in the remaining segments of this chapter and beyond.

---

our students begin to expand their beliefs about what writing is, how it can be designed, and how it can make an impact on the world. As Troy has stated with his coauthor Dawn Reed, "[d]igital writing skills are essential to the classroom as students engage in our global society" (2015, p. xxvi). Whether we realize it or not, mentor texts are all around us.

Expanding Our View of Mentor Texts

There are wonderful resources for mentor texts readily available on blogs, websites, and in professional books. One of our favorite resources is the "Mentor Text Dropbox" found on Allison Marchetti and Rebekah O'Dell's *Moving Writers* blog (the link is available at the authors' website). There you will find examples of mentor texts organized by genres and writing techniques. It is a tremendous and ever-expanding resource—one Andy leans on often.

Mentor texts can be found in countless places such as *The Atlantic*, the *New York Times*, and NPR to name a few, not to mention the many places that publish high-quality student work like the Scholastic Art and Writing Awards (the links are available at the authors' website). With so many options regarding texts as mentors, it can become a challenge to decide what to use, for what purpose, and for whom; the choices can seem overwhelming. We think Katherine Bomer offers fabulous advice when choosing mentor texts to learn from; she argues that "the texts [you] teach from in mini-lessons should be *beloved* texts so that [you] know them well and [your] enthusiasm will carry over to [your] students" (39). In the classroom, we are able to share our processes, resources, and enthusiasm in organic ways when we come across pieces that capture our imagination.

As the writing mentors in your classroom, we encourage you to seek texts that excite your imagination as a teacher-writer. Keep your eyes and ears open to what you see and hear around you for inspiration. How might you use podcasts like NPR's *The Moth*, Aaron Mahnke's *Lore*, or Sarah Koenig's *Serial* as mentor texts to showcase powerful storytelling techniques? How might you lean on TED Talks or Pecha Kuchas as compelling informative or argumentative texts? How might exciting, and Pulitzer Prize–winning, multimedia features like the *New York Times*'s "Snow Fall: The Avalanche at Tunnel Creek" encourage us to synthesize multiple

TABLE 3.1: Questions to Consider While Exploring Mentor Texts

As a Reader	As a Writer	Planning Your Writing Moves
What did you notice?	What did the writer choose to include?	What topic are you choosing to explore? Which moves are required for emulation?
What pulled you into the piece?	What did the writer choose to leave out?	
What surprised you about the approach?	Which moves did you find compelling?	How will your approach be similar to or different from the texts you have read?
What drew your attention away? Why?	What surprised you about the approach?	How will you decide what to include and what to leave out?
What do you connect with? Where do you see yourself in the text?	What was done well? Explain the effect.	
Are there any common threads you noticed within the "fabric" of these texts?	What are the moves you want to emulate?	How do you plan on structuring your piece?
What do you, as a reader, want to know more about?	Are there any common threads you noticed within the "fabric" of these texts?	Which writing moves will you include? Why?
	What do you, as a writer, want to know more about?	What are the moves you will stay away from? Explain.

**BOX 3.4: Composing Occurs in Different
            Modalities and Technologies**

It is becoming increasingly prevalent in content-area standards for English as well as in our professional standards for the preparation of teachers that we must teach students how to compose digital texts. As NCTE in *Professional Knowledge* states, "In order to provide high-quality writing opportunities for all students, teachers need to understand . . . design and layout principles for print and digital publication." Sometimes we encourage all our students to create texts in a digital form (such as a podcast or infographic), and sometimes we welcome them to explore these modalities and technologies to come up with an approach that works for them and the composition at hand.

---

modes of writing in a coauthored digital piece? Links to all these mentor texts are on this chapter's web page on the authors' website).

To put a more practical, concise spin on it, when a mentor text inspires it also creates questions in the mind of a reader as she starts to think as a writer. Texts can invite a writer to ask questions like those in Table 3.1.

A decision to write produces questions only the writer can answer. Often, questions of length, topic, requirements, standards, expectations, and personal experiences with writing amplify the voice of the inner critic and stop writers before they even begin. The fear of unknown outcomes, audience response, and anticipated results shuts down many writers. Mentor texts help to dim the volume of the inner critic, and the questions that writers ask of texts can break large writing projects into manageable chunks. As teacher-writers and students become accustomed to viewing texts with a writer's eye, they become confident in the rhetorical moves that move them beyond formulaic writing like the five-paragraph essay.

While we believe that mentor texts boost confidence in student writers, we also believe that the mentor in the room—you—emboldens student writers when you let the enthusiasm you have for a new project, idea, or piece of writing lead the way. When you are excited about the moves that make you pause in admiration, it is reflected in your teaching as well. The activities we share in this chapter are examples of mentor texts that build confidence in what we can learn from studying the moves of other writers and how they can be transferred to our students.

Writing Activities that Explore Mentor Texts

With the activities described here, we show how our third principle of encouragement comes through the exploration of mentor texts; students are, indeed, mentor text explorers. We begin in the familiar territory of letting traditional texts guide student writing and, subsequently, share examples that incorporate public speaking and digital multimodal texts that we can learn a lot from when their voices enter the conversation.

ACTIVITY 3.1:

Answering the Call: Writing Guest Blog Posts for the Nerdy Book Club

When we choose to head into the unknown, there are mentors to guide us. Although the process, in many cases, is similar, not all writing opportunities are created equal, and the perception of risk varies depending on the writing project. For example, depending on the writer's experience, anxiety levels vary when the decision is made to publish a blog post, submit a poem to a contest, or write a book. Still, the writing anxieties students might experience decrease when they read mentor texts through the eyes of a writer.

As part of a culminating feature of the Trending Topics activity in Chapter 1, Andy's students are encouraged to answer the call for guest bloggers on the Nerdy Book Club (the link is available at, the authors' website). In this space, guest bloggers are asked to share potential posts that offer book recommendations that celebrate diversity, embrace inclusivity, and are balanced in approach. These reminders to guest bloggers share insight into what the Nerdy Book Club editors value and what readers expect. In their call for guest bloggers titled "Want to Be a Nerdy Blogger?" editors describe five different types of posts:

- Reading Lives (for books that impact lives)
- New Book Reviews (for books within eighteen months of publication)
- Retro Reviews (for books published more than eighteen months ago)

- Pay It Forward (posts about promoting the love of reading)
- Top Ten (listicle posts about ten books or ten things about books)

Each type of guest blog invitation is open-ended to encourage a range of responses. So, as they read, Andy asks students to consider two questions: "What do you like as a reader?" and "What do you notice about the moves the author makes?" Students share noteworthy features, thus thinking about the moves they could use to pull readers into their post. Students learn that understanding one's audience is a hallmark of good writing. Across the five different kinds of posts, the features they share are consistent, so choosing one of the five topics then leads into a protocol for further responses that include:

- Post titles that urge readers to read the post;
- Pictures of (or from) the book (or books);
- Personal connections to the book and how books can change lives;
- Variety in sentence and paragraph length;
- Conversational tone and informal voice;
- Short author bio with name, hometown, and interests.

One of Andy's students, Haylee, chose to respond to the call for guest bloggers by writing a "Top Ten" post about books she titled "Top Ten LGBTQ+ YA Novels for All Tastes" (Geisthardt, 2018). Based on other examples of top ten lists, she prefaced the list with a personal note to her readers, "As a queer teenager, LGBTQ+ representation is especially important to me. Luckily, if you know where to look in YA lit, you can find characters all over the LGBTQ+ spectrum traversing many genres and having their experiences represented in a lot of ways." As an avid reader, Haylee wanted to share with her readers the many different ways queer representation occurs in books. Taking a cue from other mentor texts, she found that lists which grabbed her attention used an informal voice as well as an interesting synopsis of a book. Consider her take on *I'll Give You the Sun* by Jandy Nelson (2015):

> *If you haven't read this book yet, please, do so immediately.*
> *Noah's story starts when he and his twin sister Jude are thir-teen and nearly inseparable. Woven between, though, is Jude's per-spective— three years later. At sixteen Noah and Jude, separated by tragedy, are very different than before. This book tells an incredible,*

intriguing story that draws you in and never lets go. It's one of my favorites ever. It's a love story, a family story, an exploration of sexuality, a story of friendship and growth, and a philosophical journey. This book will change your life.

Moreover, Haylee became a mentor for others as her post garnered some recognition by Nerdy Book Club readers. Though surprised by the response, she was thrilled to learn she had an audience that was interested in her perspective. One reader-sought book suggestions from Haylee for a sixth grade student who was beginning to question her sexual orientation and was interested in finding herself in a book. Haylee was able to engage with her own reader, replying enthusiastically, "It really means a lot for young people like us to have the support of people like you!"

In the minds of many students, in order to be considered a writer you must be published, and if you are not, then the title of "writer" seems to be uncomfortable to claim. When Haylee opened the email confirmation that her post was accepted for publication on the Nerdy Book Club, her response surprised us and herself. She shouted "YES!" and threw her arms in the air, unable to contain her excitement. Her reaction was priceless, and we celebrated her success with a rousing chorus of snaps. And, although invitations to be guest bloggers are infrequent, in Andy's classroom they are powerful forms of recognition that no amount of teacher feedback,

---

BOX. 3.5: Flexibility and Curiosity

Writing for an authentic audience helped Haylee experience flexibility as a writer who, as the *Framework* describes, "adapt[ed] to situations, expectations, or demands" as she "reflect[ed] on the choices [she made] in light of context, purpose, and audience." And the curiosity she employed in the process let her "communicate [her] findings in writing to multiple audiences inside and outside school using discipline-appropriate conventions."

Moreover, the experience encouraged Haylee's knowledge of conventions as she needed to "write, read, and analyze a variety of texts from various disciplines and perspectives in order to . . . practice different conventions and analyze expectations for and effect on different audiences."

classroom recitations, or grade can equal. There are many other options for publication, too, shared on the authors' website.

Exploring mentor texts with a writer's eye paved the way for Haylee and her classmates to be comfortable enough to answer the guest blogger call. She was able to understand the needs of Nerdy Book Club readers and blend them with her personal purpose for writing. The act of submitting a piece for publication is fear-inducing for many writers, but it is a risk that writers must be willing to take. Writing for authentic audiences, interacting with them, and seeing the good a writer's words can do in the world is a tangible boost in confidence that no amount of peer feedback, teacher praise, or high grade can accurately measure.

ACTIVITY 3.2:
Pecha Kucha–Style Talks

When students read and write what interests them, they want to talk about it and, when encouraged, listen to others. At the end of a trimester, Andy asks his students to create and compose Pecha Kucha presentations as a fun way to share what they have learned from independently reading choice books, connections they have made to other texts, and insights gained during the course of studying their topic. Troy created a similar opportunity for his CMU freshmen, and they documented their inquiry and learning about leading a more informed digital life, both personally and academically.

Invented by architects Astrid Klein and Mark Dytham, these fun talks were created to speed up project pitches because, in their words, "give a microphone and some images to an architect—or most creative people for that matter—and they'll go on forever!" (Klein Dytham Architecture, n.d.). Again, Pecha Kucha 20x20 is a simple presentation format where presenters show 20 images, each for 20 seconds. The images advance automatically, and presenters talk along with the images. It is a presentation format that asks students to speak and listen in short bursts, relying on striking images and informed content knowledge delivered in a concise manner. There are similar presentations in style, structure, and form called Lightning Talks or Ignite Talks, but Andy prefers the Pecha Kuchas because the name itself piques students' interest.

Over the course of the second trimester, students dig in and become experts in their chosen topics. From a certain slant, it seems that encouraging students to share their learning via presentations removes them from a process of writing, but in his book *Why They Can't Write* (2018), John Warner reminds us that "by allowing students to be experts—not just content experts but also presentation experts—[teachers] fade into the background as [students] take charge of their own writing" (p. 175). Presentations allow students to enter into a process of writing that shakes up their notion of what writing can be in order to communicate an idea. It is often a welcome change of pace; still, they need classroom space and time to develop their independent reading talk. Andy creates the space they need the week before their final exam and opens up the writing workshop to give students room to focus on composing their presentations.

To help students get their bearings with this, usually unfamiliar, presentation form, he conducts a short mini-lesson using Ellen Finkelstein's "How to Create Slides" Pecha Kucha (2013). While students watch, Andy asks them to write down any moments that resonate with them regarding slide design. The experience also introduces students to what a Pecha Kucha is, the format and, at times, the nature of it. When finished, Andy asks his students to chat at their tables about what they noticed regarding Finkelstein's presentation. They notice some clear protocols for an effective talk:

- Slides have few, if any words, and usually for effect;
- Slides have a central, guiding image;
- Image and text placement are strategic;
- The talk itself is rehearsed but not stilted;
- Speakers employ humor and empathy.

To further this point, instead of leaning on presenters with years of experience in front of an audience, Andy shares the recorded work of former students, which he has saved on YouTube in a "Best of Pecha Kucha" playlist (link on the authors' website). These (former) students demonstrate expectations outlined in the project through their actual performance, and (current) students can openly discuss the moves, in both presentation style and slide design, that they find interesting, intriguing, or to be avoided altogether.

Lily Wagner, having the opportunity to read texts of her choice—in this case, *Madame Bovary* by Gustave Flaubert (1856) and *The Picture of Dorian Gray* by Oscar Wilde (1890)—on a topic of her choice, "The Consequences of Vanity" (2019, linked on the authors' website), took advantage of the informal Pecha Kucha structure to push her own thinking about craft, design, and structure. In her talk, she drew from a number of pieces of art to illustrate her ideas from the canonical books, tying together ideas related to vanity and making connections to modern celebrities and social media.

She begins her talk by arguing that "[v]anity is really treasured nowadays. We follow celebrities who post only the best things about their lives." She then moves quickly (as the Pecha Kucha style requires!) into connections to Greek mythology, as well as her own analysis of *Madame Bovary* and *Dorian Gray*. By the end, she acknowledges that some vanity is useful and that self-love is important. However, "there's a damaging point, there's a thin line" where it becomes destructive. Though her slides finished a few seconds earlier than she may have wished, Lily is able to tie things together with grace and humor.

As we continue to think about ways mentor texts (digital or otherwise) create confident writers, let's not forget the mentor texts created within the walls of our own classrooms. For many students it is intimidating to try to write up to the level of professional writers. When teachers rely only on those texts, we may inadvertently amplify feelings generated by imposter syndrome, a feeling of inadequacy or potential failure. Finally, student-

---

BOX 3.6: Flexibility and Openness

The use of professional and student digital mentor texts provided the flexibility Lily needed to, as described in the *Framework*, "reflect on the choices [she made] in light of context, purpose, and audience." Moreover, she demonstrated an openness to experiment with an unfamiliar presentation style that allowed her to "practice different ways of gathering, investigating, developing, and presenting information." The experience encouraged Lily's critical thinking, too, as she aimed to "craft written responses to texts that put the writer's ideas in conversation with those in a text in ways that are appropriate to the academic discipline or context."

created digital mentor texts enhance engagement of a seemingly daunting challenge because they are witness to others, peers of their age and of their ability, producing short and provocative presentations. In this way, students are likely to organically raise the stakes and exceed the expectations of a project with some positive peer pressure.

ACTIVITY 3.3:
Digital Mentors and Multimedia Texts

As you have read throughout the chapter, we fully support the practice of using mentor texts encouraging students to analyze traditional texts by answering the question: What did the writer do? In our digital age, though, it begs the question: What of digital texts? No doubt students are inundated with texts that flash across the screens that are in their pockets, on their walls, and even at the gas pumps. Digital texts are everywhere, yet we aren't doing enough to teach our students how to create them, for what purpose, and for whom. Common Sense Media's most recent report, *The Common Sense Census: Inside the 21st-Century Classroom*, paints a stark picture:

> *Teachers place a high value on digital creation tools in developing 21st-century skills, but these tools are among the least used in the classroom . . . While productivity and presentation tools were used in about half of classrooms, digital creation tools were only used in 25 percent of classrooms. (Vega & Robb, 2019, p. 8)*

Both Andy and Troy use multimedia as mentor texts. For instance, with the various project pathways that students can pursue in Troy's class, they can look at websites, podcasts, videos, interactive maps, timelines, infographics, and even a genre of "how to" instructions. By providing students with various project pathways as well as technologies from which they can choose to represent their ideas, students have many options to consider and build from.

3.3.1:
Multimedia Journalism as a Mentor Text

For Andy, it is the *New York Times*'s "Snow Fall: The Avalanche at Tunnel Creek" that provides a compelling multimedia mentor text (2012). Author John Branch and the *Times* multimedia team create a unique experience for readers by weaving in multimodal texts, telling the harrowing tale of a group of experienced skiers who find themselves at the mercy of an avalanche as they describe their purpose for the trip, their experiences, and the survival stories. It is an amazing experience for readers and an intriguing opportunity for student writers—well worth your time to explore (the link is available at the chapter page on the authors' website).

Andy explains that students will be examining the role and purpose of place on people and that they will be using "Snow Fall" as a way to jump-start their thinking about the choices the authors made in creating the text. He asks students to make a basic T-Chart (dividing their pages in half with room for headings at the top) in their writers' notebooks or on a Google Doc and write down what they notice about the text. In the buzz of conversation, he hears students talk about the close-up view of the GIF used as wind blows a trace amount of snow from left to right down an incline. They talk about the placement of the title and the font used. One student recognizes that the narrative begins with the climax, the avalanche itself, and the piece centers itself around that environmental event. Students appreciate short, yet powerful, video interviews with survivors like Elyse Saugstad, who recalls the sensation of being swept away in the avalanche. Each group marvels at the sweeping Google Earth video of the landscape surrounding Tunnel Creek. Finally, one student verbalizes what everyone in the room is thinking: "That is so cool! How did they do that?"

This inquiry opens up the conversation to consider the moves made by the *New York Times* contributors. Andy shares a *Source* article titled "How We Made Snow Fall" (Duenes et al., n.d.). The article digs into an in-depth series of specific questions and answers detailing how the *New York Times* team—a writer, a video journalist, and a graphics editor—worked together from fuzzy concept to astonishing composition. Branch explains how their team used multiple modes of writing to integrate the graphics and video into the narrative experience:

> The key was the cooperation of those involved. Every one of them opened his or her heart to me, a stranger with only a loose idea of where the story might head. They were honest and gracious and trusting. And when I returned with their stories, and we saw how their various perspectives of the same avalanche wove together, we invited the smart people in our interactive and graphics departments to help with the telling. (2013)

Students soon recognize that this is no ordinary group project. Instead of the familiarity of splitting up roles and collaborating to create a traditional piece of writing, students are asked to focus first on a climactic weather event, like the avalanche in "Snow Fall," that could serve as an extended metaphor. Then they use their chosen extended metaphor as the center of a digital multimodal piece as they craft, individually and divergently, a website from the various writing lenses of traditional narrative, video journalism, and graphics editing. The result is a true team effort in which students are equally dependent on one another to read, note, plan, confer, reflect, collaborate, write, and share in order to create an intriguing and literacy-rich interactive reading experience. Having archived a few examples of previous student work, Andy directs them to additional student-made projects (for links, see this chapter's page on the authors' website).

Using multimedia as professional and peer mentor texts offers teachers flexibility in how we view traditional group writing projects, such as this one, inviting us to alter group work in authentic and dynamic ways. The *New York Times* team each took on diverse roles as writers (in both the traditional and the digital sense), and during a class discussion, Andy's students identify three distinct roles: writer, video journalist, and graphic designer. Or, as Troy notes in *Crafting Digital Writing* (2013), we want students to think "like artists, designers, recording engineers, photographers, and filmmakers" (p. 19). Following the makeup of the *New York Times* team, Andy asks that students form their own teams with no more than five members and suggests that each team include a wild-card role so that they have a member who feels comfortable moving fluidly from role to role where and when needed.

Understanding that the *New York Times* journalists found themselves in those positions because of interest and talent, Andy asks students to take a few minutes to recognize the talent in the room. Students are generally quick to claim talent for the roles of video journalism and graphic designer, but many struggle with owning the talent they have as writers. Andy addresses this by acknowledging the difficulty writers have with claiming their own talent. He tells students that, though recognizing your own talent is awkward at times, others are quick to acknowledge the talented writers in their midst. Once students find a role they are comfortable with, Andy asks writers, video journalists, graphic designers, and wild cards to each move to a corner of the classroom. Here students can visually see who is in each role, and they choose teams of 4 or 5 students they will be working with on the project.

At this point Andy describes the topic of "The Role and Purpose of Place on People" and asks students to choose from Zora Neale Hurston's *Their Eyes Were Watching God* (1937), Chinua Achebe's *Things Fall Apart* (1958), Paulo Coelho's *The Alchemist* (1988), and Hermann Hesse's *Siddhartha* (1922). Just as "Snow Fall" is centered around an environmental event, an avalanche, that impacted the lives of the skiers at Tunnel Creek, these novels contain environmental events in their own right that shape, shift, and sculpt the lives of the characters in moving ways. The novels serve as the story that groups will capture as they emulate the rhetorical moves made by Branch and his team in their breathtaking digital text.

BOX 3.7: Openness and Engagement

The examination of a digital multimedia piece and the subsequent collaboration on their own website in response to literature both required openness from students in order to, in what the *Framework* describes, "practice different ways of gathering, investigating, developing, and presenting information"; it also encouraged them to "act upon the new knowledge they have discovered." Moreover, the process had students composing in multiple environments to "analyze situations where print and electronic texts are used, examining why and how people have chosen to compose using different technologies."

Of course, with any attempt using mentor texts as guides, student results vary, but we celebrate the value of experimenting, risking, and taking on a unique challenge—in this case, exploring the experiences of characters in a novel through the lens of an extended metaphor and multimodal texts. Students look at the intersections of the content (text, video, image, graphics) and the style (color, position), fully embracing the MAPS heuristic (mentioned in Chapter 2) and considering possibilities for writing that are, for most of the students, innovative and unfamiliar. Additional resources related to Andy's most recent iteration of this project, "Why Am I Here? Examining the Role of Place and Purpose on People"—including a project overview, specific steps and job assignments, and the instructions for a final gallery walk—can be found on this chapter's page on the authors' website.

3.3.2:
Vlogs and Maps as Mentor Texts

Another possible pathway that students could pursue involved the pursuit of place, an "Adventurer" pathway that would take them into the local community and focus their research on a particular theme. In the spirit of travel writing, students were invited to investigate their local community, but do so with a distinct perspective. As with the examples from Julia and Lori earlier, Taylor Gritzmaker and her group set about the task of documenting a weekend in Mount Pleasant, the community that is home to Central Michigan University, as newcomers to the town.

They, too, push the boundaries on modes and media. Taylor's group combined two forms of media: the Story Map, first mentioned in Chapter 2, and a vlog. Vlogging, as defined by Susan Gunelius of *Lifewire*, usually involves "creating a video of yourself or an event, uploading it to the internet, and publishing it within a post on your blog" (2019). Their video, "Mastering Mount Pleasant," documented in vlog-style Taylor's adventures with a classmate as they explored many eateries and local attractions.

From the first page, The Story Map shows a bit of Taylor's personality, as she demonstrates a keen sense of audience while composing the cover page for her group's Story Map. She noted in her final reflection that:

I chose to use a strategy of writing through lack of punctuation, capital letters, and using specific information such as facts that younger people would be interested in as well as relate it back to the authors through including what we tried at each place.

Using the Story Map itself, with information about each location, as well as a photo they had taken, they then explored the local community and shared their perspectives on the businesses they found. Using visually persuasive techniques in the vlog such as close-ups and slow motion, Taylor and her classmates provided a glimpse into nine local attractions, some of which their first-semester classmates still had not explored.

Describing her technique, Taylor noted:

Finally, this project hid the information and persuasion through the very obvious form of entertainment through the vlog. We were goofy, we showed our personalities and quirks, all through creating a "story" of all the things we suggest doing over a weekend in Mt. Pleasant.

In lieu of a traditional travel essay, by combining still images and video, texts and an interactive map, Taylor and her group were able to document their experiences in a compelling manner.

FIGURE 3.1: Screenshots from Taylor's Story Map and Vlog

Conclusion

Writers are inspired by what they see in the world around them. In this chapter, we have shared specific examples of how we can use mentor texts to invite, encourage, and celebrate both traditional and digital texts. Although the concept of using mentor texts to create confident writers is not new, we propose broadening the traditional view of mentor texts to incorporate authentic experiences, oral presentations, digital media, and digital multimodal texts.

When we consider the ways in which we encourage our writers to identify, attain, and consider mentor texts, we move into some uncomfortable areas. It is, without a doubt, challenging for us as teachers to move from traditional modes of using mentor texts, because of our memories of collegiate expectations. Moreover, finding ways to create spaces for engaging examples of mentor texts within the boundaries of curriculum, standardized testing, and district and university missions can, at times, seem challenging. Yet it is within these challenging spaces and times that we must consider how we explore mentor texts, for what purpose, and for whom.

- How might you model, demonstrate, or share alternative and engaging mentor texts with your students?
- In what ways could you help students expand their definition of a text? How might leaning on a broader definition of a text help create confident readers and writers?
- While we are all expected to teach certain curriculum, texts, and skills, with which of these do you have some flexibility that, in turn, you might work with your students to discover inspiring alternative and digital mentor texts?
- With digital writing, what additional digital genres might we deconstruct in order to take advantage of moves these writers make to encourage students to share their ideas with a wider audience?

CHAPTER 4

Responding to Reading

"I learned more about myself as a reader than I have at any time in recent memory. My goal is to continue to have some kind of book that I'm making my way through at all times."

—Owen Smith, MPHS

Responding to Reading Creates Confident Writers by . . .

- Connecting the reading and writing process in authentic ways;
- Acknowledging student interests through choice of topic and response style;
- Utilizing digital tools to maintain reading momentum as students capture noteworthy moments;
- Continuing to welcome them into academic conversations with published authors and peers.

Writers need to read.

This truism has been shared by many teachers and researchers who work in the broad field of literacy studies, and it has been echoed already in the works we've cited in earlier chapters. Kylene Beers and Bob Probst (2017), Penny Kittle and Kelly Gallagher (2018), and Donalyn Miller and Colby Sharp (2018)—among dozens of other voices—have guided our thinking about when, why, and how kids can be invited to read. Another voice in that conversation is Pam Allyn, the founder of LitWorld, a global organization dedicated to literacy learning in local communities and building on the strength of children's own stories (link on the authors' website).

While she is referring to work with younger students and children's literature, we think that Allyn's perspective on the role of reading in the life of a writer is clear, succinct, and useful. She argues that, by engaging in meaningful reading experiences, "Children breathe in the big ideas, people, places, and facts and breathe out their own ideas, theories, and opinions in response" (2015). We've heard variations of this idea, noting that reading is like inhaling, writing like exhaling. In rhythm, reading and writing work together, especially when approached with intention.

In her book *Writing Down the Bones* (2010), writing consultant Natalie Goldberg contends, "If you read good books, when you write, good books will come out of you." Though the process seems simple enough, she continues by acknowledging that:

> . . . maybe it's not quite that easy, but if you want to learn something, go to the source . . . Dogen, a great Zen master, said, "If you walk in the mist, you get wet." So just listen, read, and write. Little by little, you will come closer to what you need to say and express it through your voice. (p. 67)

Reading, in this metaphor, helps us get a little wet. Thus, in a book focused primarily on the teaching of writing, where we are inviting, encouraging, and cele-

---

BOX 4.2: Writing Is a Tool for Thinking

Encouraging students to respond to their reading builds on many of the habits of mind presented in the *Framework*, notably that of "curiosity," as students "seek relevant authoritative information and recognize the meaning and value of that information." We also see the reading/writing relationship as one that produces "engagement," as students "make connections between their own ideas and those of others."

Moreover, as the NCTE *Professional Knowledge* reminds us: "In order to provide high-quality writing opportunities for all students, teachers need to understand . . . when writers actually write, they think of things that they did not have in mind before they began writing. The act of writing generates ideas; writing can be an act of discovery."

brating the ways in which students write, we also know that we must do all of this in the service of their reading lives, too. So, as we consider what could happen in high school and college classrooms, we feel that reading can play an even more critical role. Creating confident writing requires that we, as teachers of writing, invite, encourage, and celebrate students' response to reading.

We encourage you to join us in collegial conversation about approaches to writing, this time focused on responding to reading. When teaching writing, we consider these questions:

- Through the classroom habits we embrace, do we encourage our students to grow by creating predictable routines for independent reading?
- Through writing experiences we offer, do we emphasize a process of responding to texts that increases students' opportunities to write and increases the complexity of that writing?
- By introducing students to literary lenses, do we help students envision multiple perspectives in response to a text and encourage them to choose a lens that interests them?
- Over the course of a trimester or semester, do we encourage students to engage in a variety of forms of reading response that include writing-to-learn, peer-to-peer talk, class-wide conversations, teacher conferences, and multimodal expression?

Reading: An Entry Point for Writers into Larger Conversations

To create confident writers, we need to open up conversation in the classroom. It means we have to invite students to take a seat at the table and center conversations around reading texts that encourage students to weigh in. As students become comfortable sharing their ideas in response to texts, either verbally or as they write, they build their confidence and begin to see themselves as worthy contributors to larger conversations. One way to think about the importance of conversation is to consider a metaphor from a writer and rhetorician.

American literary theorist Kenneth Burke understood and encouraged the reciprocal nature of reading and writing. He shared the idea not only to help students improve their writing but also to help them see their ideas are part of a much larger ongoing conversation. In his work *The Philosophy of Literary Form* (1974),

Burke described his idea of an "unending conversation" by asking writers to engage in an extended metaphor:

> *Imagine that you enter a parlor. You come late. When you arrive, others have long preceded you, and they are engaged in a heated discussion, a discussion too heated for them to pause and tell you exactly what it is about. In fact, the discussion had already begun long before any of them got there, so that no one present is qualified to retrace for you all the steps that had gone before. You listen for a while, until you decide that you have caught the tenor of the argument; then you put in your oar. Someone answers; you answer him; another comes to your defense; another aligns himself against you, to either the embarrassment or gratification of your opponent, depending upon the quality of your ally's assistance. However, the discussion is interminable. The hour grows late, you must depart. And you do depart, with the discussion still vigorously in progress. (pp. 110–11)*

Becoming comfortable entering into conversations requires student writers to know enough about their topic to give them something to talk about. Each unfamiliar topic that students encounter brings with it an unforeseen barrier as they learn to trust themselves enough to take those first tentative steps into a larger conversation they feel they are able and, in some cases, knowledgeable enough to take part in. Within these conversations, students are able to gain confidence in their writing when they see their ideas add value to larger ideas.

With that in mind, we opt for experiences based on inquiry stances that result in texts and perspectives students are more interested in exploring. Students who are encouraged to read texts to inform their own questions develop healthy reading relationships because they want to learn more about the topics they choose. Advocates of student choice have long recognized that students are motivated to read and write when they have options that appeal to them. When we empower students to have control over their learning, they are more likely to respond to reading with depth and clarity. To help students capitalize on their intrinsic motivation, Andy asks students to find texts that pull them in. As students read what speaks to them, their desire to read, and subsequently write, generates organically.

In his classes, Andy encourages his students to build meaningful reading habits by choosing texts they have no choice but to fall in love with. For example, when he asks students to choose books for independent reading, he asks them to look for books that they want to have a relationship with. These relationships should not be

BOX 4.3: Critical Thinking

As the critical thinking section of the *Framework* suggests, students should "read texts from multiple points of view (e.g., sympathetic to a writer's position and critical of it) and in ways that are appropriate to the academic discipline or other contexts where the texts are being used." This is a key aspect of reading like a writer, a skill we want our students to employ as they examine mentor texts.

forced. Andy asks them to seek books that pull them in, and, as Penny Kittle suggests in *Book Love: Developing Depth, Stamina, and Passion in Adolescent Readers* (2013), he, too, encourages them to break off a relationship with a book where it feels as though they are just slogging through it. Andy tells his students that there are too many good books in the world to waste time in a one-sided relationship. When they know what they like to read, they discover voices they enjoy writing in.

Though Andy shares a variety of ways to respond to readings, he believes students have options when it comes to choosing how they want to record their thinking. He demonstrates and helps students find a balance between traditional and digital note-taking methods. As he encourages students to explore these different methods, he ultimately wants them to discover which note-taking methods work best for them. While not meant to be an exhaustive list, Table 4.1 shows multiple

TABLE 4.1: Traditional and Digital Methods of Responding to Reading

MINI-LESSONS: WRITING IN RESPONSE TO READING	
Traditional	**Digital**
• Marginalia	• Notes app on phone
• T-Charts	• #BookSnaps with phone camera
• Sticky notes	• Google Slides
• White board	• Google Docs
• Sketch notes	• Voice memo app
• Notebooks	• Flipgrid
• Peer feedback	• Forums
• Structuring a draft	• Blog posts
• Quick writes	• Collaborative documents

BOX 4.4: Writing Is a Tool for Thinking

With each of these activities, whether done in short, in-class bursts or across class sessions, Andy invites his students to use writing as a tool for thinking. NCTE makes the point in *Professional Knowledge* that "[i]n order to provide high-quality writing opportunities for all students, teachers need to understand . . . how to employ varied tools for thinking through writing, such as journals, writers' notebooks, blogs, sketchbooks, digital portfolios, listservs or online discussion groups, dialogue journals, double-entry or dialectical journals, and others." We believe that purposeful response to reading boosts confidence in student writers. Moreover, we believe there are some promising practices writers employ to maintain both reading and writing momentum.

---

ways in which Andy uses mini-lessons to demonstrate written response options. By demonstrating a variety of ways to respond in writing to reading, Andy encourages his students to discover their *own* way to record, curate, and respond to reading, not the *only* way to do it.

Just as each writer has their own preference for a writing medium, each will come to discover through trial and error the methods they prefer to capture thoughts, gather ideas, and curate their findings while reading. Andy is interested in his students finding their way as they build confident writing identities. He recognizes, in his own writing life, that his responses to reading depend on his purpose for writing, and he believes his students should discover what works best for them. The activities we share in this chapter are examples of written responses (both traditional and digital) to reading that build confidence in writers.

Writing Activities that Encourage Response to Reading

As we consider the many ways in which students can engage in reading, a few activities described here show how our fourth principle, responding to reading, works to build confidence. We begin with low-stakes, informal responses in #BookSnaps; move to quick writes that deepen thinking and open conversations; and progress all the way up to a formal essay with literary theory as a driving force for making an academic argument.

ACTIVITY 4.1:
#BookSnaps

Reading and responding to texts, while part of what we must do in English class, remains challenging if we want to maintain joyful reading. On the one hand, we want students to read texts of their choice that pull them into the reading; we want them to build relationships with books. On the other hand, we are also interested in creating opportunities for students to engage in meaningful conversations around the texts they read; we want them to talk about books. Unfortunately, when we ask them to gather information, ideas, and citations, that process can unintentionally strip away the joy of reading.

Choosing books. Talking about books. Writing about books. We would hope this would be a natural part of students' reading lives. In order to help readers stay engaged with the texts they are reading, Andy invites his students to, yes, use the technology they have in their pockets. While classroom conversations are important, there are times when a close reading of a specific passage of text is critical. Indeed, as Troy and his colleague Kristen Hawley Turner argue in *Connected Reading* (2015), "Digital annotation allows those shared readings to live on the screen indefinitely," extending beyond the conversations that happen in the classroom (p. 87). By using the technology, we as teachers can help students respond to reading in innovative and productive ways.

Using a variation of Tara Martin's #BookSnaps (2016), in which readers use filters, texts, emojis, and bitmojis to "create a digital visual representation of the text along with the annotation," the idea is to capture a reader response in Snapchat or a built-in photo app. With a mind toward maintaining a reader's flow, Andy asks students to pay attention to the beautiful words and moments in the text, appreciating the story or argument as well as the author's craft. When they experience an "aha" moment, students snap a picture of the page (including the page number) and continue reading, minimizing the interruption of their reading flow. Students follow this pattern of taking a picture and continuing to read, and this could happen during independent reading time in class or outside of class.

At whatever point the group reconvenes—perhaps before the end of the class period, perhaps the next day—Andy invites the individuals exploring the different books to talk with each other reading the same text in small groups, sharing their initial images, holding up their phones to share while talking about their reactions. Some students may have only one image, while others may take five or six. So long as they have something, even one thing, that resonated for them from what they have read, they can enter the conversation. For about five minutes, each group is able to peruse their initial pictures and, when they have found the picture that resonates most for the individual reader or for the group as a whole, they begin to annotate.

Though students are quite capable of adding emojis, applying filters, and otherwise annotating the images of the book's pages, the first time they engage in this activity, early in the trimester, Andy offers a quick mini-lesson on the "Book, Head, Heart" framework (Beers & Probst, 2017) as an intellectual lens through which to consider their trending topics reading (introduced in Chapter 1). During the mini-lesson, he reminds students that the #BookSnaps they take should be relevant to the topic they are exploring. At that point, students are then able to share their annotated #BookSnaps with their small groups.

It is worth noting that these moments could be a point at which students would post their snaps to social media, as Tara Martin suggests, or share through the class management system, like Google Classroom. Whether students choose to share them beyond their small groups or not, many times students save these images for their final reflection, too.

As noted in earlier chapters, Andy's students had already spent time identifying their trending topics, and one student was particularly interested in the idea of injustice; she wanted to read *The Hate U Give* as part of this inquiry. Sarah Meadows wanted to better understand the experiences of African Americans, the role of racial profiling, and, she was keenly interested in Angie Thomas's book. It is worth taking a moment to visit our website, <hickstro.org/confidentwriters>, to see exactly what she created before reading our impressions of Sarah's #BookSnaps. In her snaps, she used blue, black, and pink to represent her reactions to the "book," "head," and "heart," respectively.

In this series of #BookSnaps, taken over one week, Sarah shows her increasing interest—and indignation—as she moved further and further into Starr's story. In the first #BookSnap, Sarah reacts to Khalil's shooting and tries to make sense of how African Americans are told to respond to police

FIGURE 4.1: Sarah Meadows Engaged in Reading

when pulled over and the fact that it still does not stop the violence (in her snap of page 23). As Sarah notes, "All Khalil did was check on his friend, but since he was black they thought they had a credible reason for danger." Then, later in the week and 200 pages further into the book, Sarah points out how the police seem to be more afraid of African Americans than the African American community is afraid of the police. She reflects on the ways in which black people must rely on "luck" as part of their daily lives by annotating page 220. Sarah notes that Mr. Lewis, a local barber who was attacked by the King Lords, "talked about [the incident] very casually," referencing Mr. Lewis's point that it took five gang members to subdue one old man after he had "snitched on live TV" (p. 216).

In her snap of page 246, Sarah makes a "heart" connection to the text, as indicated by the many heart emojis, but also through her terse reactions such as "shows how they [police officers] can say whatever they want even if it's not true" and "I think this is something very wrong with the system, and needs to be fixed." The heart connection she makes initially quickly turns to a "head" connection, showing the ways in which Sarah is synthesizing the themes in the book. In the final image, Sarah reflects on the ways in which African Americans must attend to speaking with the media or authorities (in her snap of page 273). In addition to seeing the many colors and copious use of star emojis, Sarah's written response shows how impassioned she was at this point in the book. Starr's father and the leader of the gang, King, are talking about Khalil and the police, and Sarah articulates the point that "they [King and Daddy] are trying to say how they [the police] always turn it to make the person [who was] killed [into] the bad guy."

So, even in these four #BookSnaps from the first half of the book, we can see how Sarah's engagement has increased as she better understands the characters and the thematic elements in *The Hate U Give*. Consider the connections Sara made while she read, as she dove into the topic of #BlackLivesMatter. Even in these four samples, and noting that Sarah took about a dozen images from the entire book, we can see that she was engaged in the underlying issues from the book, seeing Starr's perspective as she shifted back and forth between her home life, her school life, and the constant struggle of life in her community with the gangs, the police, and systematic oppression.

As a result of these low-stakes writing moments, Sarah practiced integrated note-taking habits in ways relevant to her use of technology. There is a dance, it seems, for student writers who are learning to build relationships with books as they read with writing in mind. Just as there are climactic moments that live in a dancer's memory, there are also natural moments to rest and bask in the thrilling moment on the dance floor or, in our case, in a book. By snapping a picture and, later, discussing, annotat-

---

BOX 4.5: Openness and Engagement

The *Framework*'s habit of openness to "practice different ways of gathering, investigating, developing, and presenting information" is reflected in Sarah's #BookSnaps experience. By using her smartphone, Sarah engaged with digital tools to "find meanings new to [her] or build on existing meanings as a result of new connections." This also connects to the idea that students should be composing in multiple environments, by "[using] a variety of electronic technologies intentionally to compose."

ing, and sharing even more insights, our readers are able to remember the dance steps.

These opportunities for Andy's students to fully engage with the text—and use their smartphones in equally smart ways—build their confidence as writers, providing them with textual evidence, entry points, and connections for the more substantive writing they will do later, such as guest blog posts for the Nerdy Book Club (discussed in Chapter 3) and in their Edublog Portfolio (to be discussed in Chapter 6).

ACTIVITY 4.2:
They Say / I Say Quick Writes

Building momentum for writing means creating the opportunities for students to build on their writing. When students write with a text in mind and annotate it with personal connections and questions, they begin to consider which perspectives—as Beers and Probst attest—confirm, challenge, or change their thinking on a topic. Typically, students focus their writing from one perspective: their own. But in the case of synthesizing ideas, it is useful to consider multiple perspectives. In this way students are able to negotiate their ideas about what others say on a topic in light of their current perspective.

Loosely adapted from the *They Say / I Say* sentence templates developed by Gerald Graff and Cathy Birkenstein (2018), these timed quick writes are designed to be short ten-minute burst writing sessions immediately after experiencing a text. Students find this strategy particularly useful as they write their way into their thinking. These moments to capture thinking require the writer to push past all the self-doubt simply to discover what they have to say about a text. When paired with the complex thinking required for a sustained synthesis piece, quick writes help writers think about a text without feeling the need for self-editing as they go. Students find quick-write protocols especially helpful as they explore multiple texts over a short period of time. It is worth noting that Dave Stuart Jr. has done all writing teachers a tremendous favor by capturing the entire set of sentence templates in a Google Doc, which is linked from this chapter's page on the authors' website.

After writing, Andy joins a table group (and participates with them) as students take stock of what they learned through conversation with each other. During these conversations, the students review their quick writes and share what resonated with them by discussing what confirmed, challenged, or changed their thinking (Beers & Probst, 2017). In these conversations, they can both assess what they think about the text and their thinking as well as learn how an audience might respond to their ideas. The quick feedback loop helps to build confidence in students learning to trust themselves during these short bursts before their inner judge has a chance to infiltrate their thinking.

To introduce this activity, Andy explains that they will be considering literary tragedy from multiple perspectives through the ages using a variety of texts. He adds that over the course of the study he will ask them to enter into a conversation about tragedy that has been going on since what seems like the dawn of time. To help students grapple with tragedy and the many takes on it, students create a Google Doc or dedicate space in their writers' notebooks for their quick writes. After reading, viewing, or experiencing a text that reveals a new take on literary tragedy, students engage in a ten-minute timed quick write. Andy explains to his students that, often, when we do not write about a text while we sit beside it, our responses can float away, become confused, or be muddled at times.

During the ten minutes they are quick writing, Andy asks them to write one page in response to the text. The first half of the page is dedicated to what "they say" in the text; students are meant to restate the main ideas from the literature via summary, quotation, or paraphrase—thus capturing the crux of the author's perspective. The second half of the page is their response to what they read, the "I say." Using quick writes every day for the ten days of the tragedy unit allows students to process a variety of texts, to deepen their understanding, and to develop a philosophical statement about the role of tragedy in literature, art, and culture.

For a full version of this assignment, "Tragedy Quick Write Project," the link is available at this chapter's page on the authors' website. The process that Andy and his students repeat daily as a part of their exploration of tragedy includes the following:

- Explore the texts(s) provided for 5–15 minutes, depending on the resource.
- After reading, viewing, or listening to the text(s), write for 10 minutes. In addition to writing about the guiding questions for each day's writing:
  — write 250 words of what "they say" in the text. Cite textual evidence from the tragedy you are reading (novel, poem, play, film, or other media);
  — write 250 words of what "I say" in response to the text and how it relates to your life. What interpretations can you make?
- Discuss our findings as a class (or in small groups):
  — What was compelling about this question?
  — What surprised you in the text itself, or in your own writing about the text?
  — What challenged, changed, or confirmed your thinking about tragedy as an idea/aspect of our culture?
  — Why does this matter *or* how does this connect to your evolving understandings about tragedy?

As one example, Lily Wagner, a twelfth grade student, wrote in her first response, "I've never been fond of the tragedy genre. I often feel as though my life is tragic enough and I should avoid watching others' tragedies unless some humor is involved and I can feel better about my life." Her initial response echoes the sentiment of many students who view tragedy as simply a sad story.

The next day, after a free exploration of tragedy on *Wikipedia* where students choose three specific aspects of tragedy they find compelling, Lily reported that "tragedy used to just be people of wealth and high class. Over time we've changed that definition to suit our society as it changes. It's been argued that tragedies can be about any sort of character no matter the stature or state of his or her being." A quick dip into *Wikipedia* widened her view slightly, and her response began to shift.

Over the course of the next four days, having encountered and written responses to TED Talks, literary criticism, and poetry, Andy asks students to craft and refine their working definition of literary tragedy. Lily shares her response: "tragedy is a term in which we judge a situation where humanity can triumph but the human itself may not triumph." She pauses for a moment to consider where her thinking was at the onset of the quick write process, when she wrote, "my life is tragic enough and I should avoid watching others' tragedies unless some humor is involved." Her initial surface-level thinking has deepened with a handful of quick write responses. Now, when asked to reconsider her definition of tragedy, she writes, "tragedy is something humanity can find light and learn from, and it's an event that makes us stronger. No tragedy ever keeps us stuck in one spot. It moves on from us as life goes on, but it changes the way we act every day."

In deepening her thinking about a topic she's "never really been fond of," Lily found that responding to reading with quick writes was a valuable entry point as she moved her ideas in conversation about literary tragedy. In a moment of reflection, she says, "tragedy used to be nothing but the genre of a play to me. I always thought of *Hamlet* or *Macbeth* and just assumed the story was about someone who's going through some unfortunate event and is unable to come out on top. This project opened my eyes to the complexity of what a tragedy can be and completely changed my point of view."

In Lily's case, the quick write process clarified her notion of literary tragedy. We are impressed by the results of her writing and want to share the final sentences of her philosophical reflection on literary tragedy. Through the process of reading, responding, conversing, and entering into conversation with various texts, she surmised that "a piece of literature defined as a tragedy is never truly a tragedy. It contains a tragic event

---

BOX 4.6: Metacognition and Curiosity

The quick writes helped Lily to, in the words of the *Framework*, "use what [she] learn[ed] from reflections on one writing project to improve writing on subsequent projects" and awaken her curiosity to "seek relevant authoritative information and recognize the meaning and value of that information." Additionally, Lily was developing flexible writing processes by "incorporat[ing] evidence and ideas from written, visual, graphic, verbal, and other texts."

that reveals humanity's ability to triumph even if it's not evident and takes time. Tragedies highlight the capability to move on and evolve as life continues." A link to her final essay can be found on this chapter's page on the authors' website.

Asking students to engage with short texts, both traditional and digital, side by side can stretch their notions of what writing "is," besides just being alphabetic text. Instead of reading lengthy texts while attending to many ideas that seem important in a larger picture, students are able to navigate quickly between perspectives without losing their own.

ACTIVITY 4.3:
Responding with Literary Lenses

As students build confidence by writing about and responding to texts, they become more willing when asked to move outside their comfort zones and engage with more complex texts. Traditionally, the works of William Shakespeare are among the most complex texts that students in Andy's AP Literature course encounter. Students struggle with the language, character motivations, and situational contexts, which are unfamiliar to their lives. For this reason, many students tend toward plot summary when responding to Shakespearean works (and, sadly, are enabled by dozens, if not hundreds, of sample essays and other summaries they can find online). In most cases, a student's struggles with Shakespearean drama centers on how much there is to unpack regarding the works. Shakespeare, in short, requires scaffolding. After having students begin by viewing either *Macbeth* or *King Lear* to build familiarity, Andy asks them to choose a literary lens and write a proposal, as explained in Chapter 2.

Built off an assignment about literary theory he originally found in Jim Burke's *English Teachers Companion* (2012), Andy uses Burke's guide, "The Basics: Critical Theory," with his students to explore the play of their choice as viewed through the lens they choose. Two additional resources that have been valuable for Andy and his students include "Literary Criticism: Questions for a Variety of Approaches" created by Maria Hiaasen of

Hereford High School in Parkton, Maryland (n.d.) and "Literary Theories: A Sampling of Critical Lenses" created by Rachel Cupryk of Red Mountain High School in Mesa, Arizona (n.d.). All three are available as links on the authors' website.

During a second viewing of the drama, with their paper proposals and literary theories in mind, students capture moments, scenes, speeches, soliloquies, and asides that help shed light on their critical theory. In other words, as students watch, they respond to those moments that resonate with them through the literary lens they have chosen. For example, using her postmodern lens and Cornell notes (where students split their note-taking page in half, using one column to document exactly what they see while, in the other column, generating questions and making connections), Taylor Idema developed her guiding questions as she considered her short study of postmodernism, her first viewing of *Macbeth*, and her proposed paper. She was able to bring to the surface intriguing focus questions such as:

- "What are anxieties that come with the changes that Macbeth and Lady Macbeth endure on their quest to power?"
- "How do other characters respond to Macbeth and Lady Macbeth's madness with the anxiety they produce?" and
- "What rules do we follow? The rules of our government? Or the rules of a mythological power (fate, a higher power, mythological being)?"

These potent questions gave Taylor more fuel as a writer because she was given the agency to choose three aspects of the task: a play that interested her, a literary lens that resonated with her, and the angle in which she wanted to respond to the text. In turn, this led her to craft a literary analysis titled "A Postmodern Perspective on the Achievement of Power," in which she concluded:

By analyzing both William Shakespeare's Macbeth *and some of the most influential world leaders throughout history through the lens of postmodernism, we are left with more questions than answers. Postmodernism allows for more than one truth, all depending on the perspective from which you look at an issue. So when asked the question "how do we ultimately achieve power? By fate or free*

> **BOX 4.7: Curiosity and Persistence**
>
> Taylor's curiosity enabled her to, again connecting to the *Framework*, "conduct research using methods for investigating questions appropriate to the discipline." By giving her a choice of the Shakespearean play, the literary lens, and the personal perspective or angle on the topic, Taylor was better suited to be persistent in her pursuit to "commit to exploring, in writing, a topic, idea, or demanding task." The experience enhanced Taylor's ability to develop flexible writing processes by "practicing all aspects of writing processes including invention, research, drafting, sharing with others, revising in response to review, and editing."

will?", we find the answer to be complex and multifaceted. Macbeth believed that he achieved power by succumbing to fate, but others believed his actions to be motivated by free will.

Rather than providing students with a simple template for analysis, in which they fill in the blanks with a few examples of textual evidence, this inquiry-driven approach puts them in control of their own literary interpretations.

In order to build their literary analysis, students like Taylor are asked to read and respond to complex texts in ways that honor their perspective and offer differing views. Essential to these responses are the ways in which choice engages student interest and emphasizes the importance of their voice in the larger literary conversation of, in this case, postmodernism. Complex as some readings are—and, even as teachers who have studied these texts for years, we still know that Shakespeare is difficult—when we honor students' interests, we help them find a light within a text to guide their thinking. While nearly all English teachers are required to teach some texts from the literary canon (and contemporary literature, too), the *ways* in which we teach these texts make all the difference. Though Andy's students are expected to engage with a Shakespearean drama as part of the AP curriculum, they are presented with many options about how to do so.

ACTIVITY 4.4:
Joining the Contemporary Conversation

Julia and Lori, both of whom have been mentioned earlier, teamed together again for their final project of the semester. The project pathway they chose focused on social justice and, as described on their project's home page:

> We chose this pathway because we understand the importance of education and activism on social justice issues, and we wanted to learn more [about] ourselves, our peers, and these extremely relevant issues. We hope that you can use this site as a resource to help educate yourself on social justice issues!

With a group of three other classmates, and as part of their original research for the group's work, they decided that, rather than interviewing an expert, they would instead design a survey that would be shared with other CMU students. In addition to asking students to identify some demographic information, including their religious affiliation, the Social Justice Opinion Survey then asked participants to complete two Likert scale questions related to the five issues under investigation: abortion/reproductive rights, immigration reform, healthcare reform, gun control, and LGBTQ+ education. These questions asked survey participants to provide ratings on a 5-point scale, ranging from "strongly disagree" to "strongly agree," with a neutral point in the middle.

For Lori, the process of developing the survey was particularly insightful, as she strove to help her group make sure "that the survey was as free from bias and prejudice as possible." Thus, in the design of the questions, she noted that "[m]y group members and I spent much of our class period discussing how to phrase our questions in ways that would not be misinterpreted or suggest a right answer." For instance, with the topic of immigration, two questions were framed, each with a 5-point Likert scale from "strongly disagree" to "strongly agree" as options:

- The US government currently has an efficient system for people to come into the US legally and become citizens.
- Immigrants contribute greatly to American society, culture, and economy.

After sending out their survey, and getting just over 70 responses from other CMU students, Lori and Julia's group went to work, interpreting the data and representing it in useful ways (link on this chapter's page on the authors' website).

Returning to the themes she explored in her digital identity narrative, Julia's inquiry on immigration and reform led to a final page on the social justice website that introduced a series of facts (from sources such as the Council on Foreign Relations and the Pew Research Center), an infographic, a summary of recent action on immigration, and the Social Justice Opinion Survey results. In the infographic, Julia worked to summarize the stances taken by three political parties, being careful to note the ways that Democrats, Republicans, and Libertarians "typically" might view issues related to immigration.

Julia then interpreted the findings from the poll of other students. For the two statements in her part of the survey, she discovered the results shown in

So What Do Americans Think About Immigration??

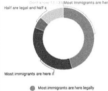

Fewer than half of Americans know that most immigrants in the U.S. are here legally. Just 45% of Americans say that most immigrants living in the U.S. are here legally; 35% say most immigrants are in the country illegally, while 6% volunteer that about half are here legally and half illegally and 13% say they don't know. (Pew Research Center)

- Most immigrants are here legally
- Most immigrants are here illegally
- Half are legal and half are illegal   - Don't know

Americans are divided on future levels of immigration. Nearly half said immigration to the U.S. should be decreased (49%), while one-third (34%) said immigration should be kept at its present level and jus 15% said immigration should be increased. (Pew Research Center)

- Immigration should be increased
- Immigration should be decreased
- Immigration should be kept at present level

Geiger, Abigail. "Key Findings about U.S. Immigrants." Pew Research Center, Pew Research Center, 30 Nov. 2018, www.pewresearch.org/fact-tank/2018/09/14/key-findings-about-u-s-immigrants/

Democrats
(Typically)

- Believe the US should enforce current border policy
- Believe sanctuary cities should be federally funded
- Support a path to citizenship for law-abiding immigrants.
- Create more ways for people to come to the United States with visas and not through smugglers.
- Support DACA/DAPA (Deferred Action for Parents of Americans)

Republicans
(Typically)

- Believe border restrictions should be increased
- Believe sanctuary cities should not be federally funded
- Oppose all forms of amnesty for unlawfully present immigrants.
- Focus on "the alarming levels of unemployment and underemployment" among citizens, rather than bringing in more immigrants
- Believe that DACA/DAPA are direct violations of federal law

Libertarians
(Typically)

- Believe that the US should have an open border policy for free flow of people, idea: goods, and services.
- Sanctuary cities should not be federally funded.
- are in favor of DACA, though they are divided on the issue

Sources

"Democratic Party on Immigration." On the Issues: Every Political Leader on Every Issue, 11 Sept. 2018, www.ontheissues.org/Celeb/Democratic_Party_Immigration.htm.
"The Political Parties Stances on Immigration." ISideWith, www.isidewith.com/political-parties/issues/immigration/immigration.
"Major Party Positions." Border Militarization Policy | National Network for Immigrant and Refugee Rights, www.nnirr.org/drupal/immigration-2016-elections-major-party-positions.

FIGURE 4.2

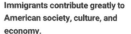

Honors Poll Results

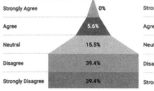

The US government currently has an efficient system for people to come into the US legally and become citizens.

Strongly Agree	0%
Agree	5.6%
Neutral	15.5%
Disagree	39.4%
Strongly Disagree	39.4%

Immigrants contribute greatly to American society, culture, and economy.

Strongly Agree	46.5%
Agree	42.3%
Neutral	11.3%
Disagree	0%
Strongly Disagree	0%

Interpretation of Results

Graph A: These results show that the sample of Honors students believe that the immigration system as it stands in the US is flawed and needs improvement. This is especially shown by 0% of the sample strongly agreeing to the statement that the US currently has an efficient system.

Graph B: It is clear that a large percentage of the students surveyed (Honors students aged 18-22) believe that immigrants make significant contributions to American society and culture.

FIGURE 4.3

Figures 4.2 and 4.3, with a clear indication that students feel the current system is inefficient and that immigrants contribute to the American economy.

As a group, Julia, Lori, and their classmates had determined that the information presented on their pages should be as neutral as possible, a conversation that had stemmed from an earlier lesson about *Wikipedia*'s neutral point of view. Instead of making a compelling argument in the form of a thesis-driven essay, they each decided to put, at the end of their issue's page, a segment titled "How you (yes you, CMU student!) can take action." For Julia, she listed four ideas that included getting educated on the topic, pursuing an "alternative break" program through the campus volunteer centers, and becoming a pen pal with refugees.

As she completed her final reflection for the course, Julia noted that the project "was time consuming, but both the increased knowledge I achieved on the issue and the research skills that I didn't know I had made it a rewarding experience."

Conclusion

In an AP Lit class, or in any English class for that matter, we can sometimes lose focus. In our efforts to look at literary devices and to check for comprehension, we forget that books are works of art and, as such, can elicit responses to reading in intellectually exciting ways. In fact, when we stop looking at books as opportunities for enjoyment and inspiration, we feel that we have lost the purpose for teaching literature. As Carol Jago reminds us, "members of a thriving community of readers are always on the lookout for something to read," and teachers have a responsibility to "maintain the pipeline of books, providing easy access to a dizzying collection of titles new and old, classic and contemporary" (2018, p. 115). After all, books, and our response to their unending conversations, offer opportunities for students to enter those conversations with the confidence needed to, as Kenneth Burke states, "put in their oar."

When we consider the ways in which we encourage our writers to respond to reading, we ask you to think of the ways you read and respond to books. What are the ways in which you enter into unending conversations? What are the topics that invigorate your thinking? How might what you read reflect what you choose to write? Here we ask you to consider your own stance on reading, as well as responding to reading. After reading the chapter, being introduced to ideas about reading response, we invite you to write, talk, and think about the following:

- Are you a reader? If you are a reader, how do you define yourself? By author(s)? Genre? Topics? What are you passionate about reading? Why? Where did this passion come from? Where is it carrying you?
- If you are not a reader, or may be an inconsistent reader, what can you do to more fully engage in a reading life? What might you need to give up in order to carve out more time for reading?
- Who are the readers in your life that you can connect to? How can they help you move forward with new authors, titles, and topics for reading?
- How might you model, demonstrate, or share your responses to reading with your students?

CHAPTER 5

Feedback and Revision

"The first piece written is not always the best and revising a piece allows me to see what areas need improvement. By going back and looking at a piece, it is like I am looking at a piece of work for the first time."

—Kayla Reihl, MPHS

Revising and Resubmitting Creates Confident Writers by . . .

- Viewing one's own writing through the eyes of a reader;
- Responding to feedback that students receive to acknowledge, consider, and explain rhetorical moves;
- Celebrating what the writer does well, acknowledging positive moments, and encouraging revision with gentle nudges;
- Utilizing digital tools to share valuable resources, revision techniques, and personalized lessons.

Writers need time to write.

For artists, a process of putting brush to canvas, throwing and molding a pot, or composing a new piece of music is the work of their craft. It is within this work and revisions that occur over time that meaning is discovered. Similarly, for writers, composing a new piece of writing, putting it away, thinking on it, digging back, crossing out, seeking feedback, and reworking is the work of their craft. Though the mediums we choose may differ, the act of creating is the same.

Like artists, writers understand the work involved in crafting, shaping, sculpting, shedding, and reworking a piece in process. This act of creating stirs up an array of emotions that run the gamut from vibrant moments of inspiration through, and including, dark-clouded moments of self-doubt. Each emotion a writer feels is normal and is part of the creative process. Still, writers know, given time and space, their writing can lead to unexpected breakthroughs. It is behind closed doors, among those they trust, where writers push up their sleeves and get to work.

Inexperienced writers, however, rarely get a glimpse behind the scenes and usually only see a finished manuscript. From this outsider's view, it seems that writing is a gift either you are born with or you are not. Experienced writers, on the other hand, recognize the need for significant time and space for revision. For many, the work begins with revision, and we need to help open the doors for our students.

As teacher-writers we value dedicated time for students to enter fully into a process of revision, because we recognize the power of entering a flow of writing. When students are working in these spaces, they, too, can enter a writing flow that is wonderful to witness. In these moments, we are at our best when we let students work without interruption. As he did throughout his life, Donald Murray gives us perspective on these powerful moments. "Revision," he contends, "can be the most satisfying part of teaching composition if the teacher is willing to let go. The composition teacher must wean the student. The teacher must give the responsibility for the text to the writer, making clear again and again that it is the student, not the teacher, who decides what the writing means" (1981, p. 34).

BOX 5.2: Writing Has a Complex Relationship to Talk

In the midst of revision, it is crucial that students have time and space to talk about their ideas. NCTE's *Professional Knowledge* reminds us that, "[i]n order to provide high-quality writing opportunities for all students, teachers need to understand . . . strategies for deliberate insertions of opportunities for talk into the writing process: knowing when and how students should talk about their writing." Doing so during the initial phases of writing is important, of course, but we are reminded that the real work of writing comes in revision, and talk should be encouraged then, too.

Indeed, it can be difficult to let go. We've both watched students struggle at times and we've seen students experience breakthroughs. We've both witnessed students spending time off-task and we've seen students collaborate as writers on their own. We've both wrestled with the decision of when to interject ideas, when to check for understanding, and when to gently nudge student attention back to the page. The writer's workshop, especially during revision, can be a messy place, and, yet, as teacher-writers we know that offering students dedicated time for purposeful revision is a hallmark of creating confident writers.

Once again, we encourage you to join us in collegial conversation about approaches to writing, this time focused on purposeful revision. When teaching writing, we consider these questions:

- Through the classroom habits we embrace, do we encourage our students to grow by offering opportunities to share our revision process?
- Through writing experiences we offer, do we emphasize a process of reenvisioning a piece to anticipate audience questions, talk about the writer's purpose, and allow for resubmission before giving a grade?
- By being responsive to students during a process of revision, do we offer adequate in-class time for a flexible and fluid workshop that encourages them to revise their work?
- Over the course of a trimester or semester, do we encourage students to revise, reshape, and resubmit pieces of their choice as many times as they would like to earn full credit?

Becoming Writers through Revision

During whole-class mini-lessons and individual conferences, there is a phrase heard often when Andy speaks to his students about writing. It is, simply, "as a writer." In his classes he asks his students, "As a writer, what jumps out to you about this piece?" He wonders with them, "How do you see yourself tackling that problem as a writer would?" He empathizes with them when they are stuck: "Isn't it frustrating, as a writer, when a piece doesn't flow the way you want? As a writer, how would you attack that problem?" He celebrates with them: "Wow! Doesn't that feel great when you make connections like that as a writer?" Andy refers to his students often as writers.

Though most of his students are on the cusp of adulthood, Andy recognizes that many still do not identify as writers and, therefore, struggle with a process of revision. Peter Johnston reminds us that "[students] are developing personal and social identities—uniquenesses and affiliations that define the people they see themselves becoming" (2004, p. 22). By referring to his students as writers, Andy helps them become comfortable identifying as writers. They view their work through the lens of a writer and, in turn, begin to internalize that language into an identity they are comfortable adopting.

Conversely, as teachers, we also begin to see them as writers, and this shifts the landscape of the classroom environment. That shift creates relationship-building opportunities for teachers, as they talk writer to writer, responding with affirmations and empathy to students still in transit. The classroom then becomes a workshop where students listen and respond to feedback through purposeful revision. This dedicated space to talk about revision opens a deeper dialogue about when, what, why, and how the work of student writers will be valued.

When the Curtain Falls:
A Critical Time for Focused Feedback

Whether we ask students to compose TED-style talks or Pecha Kucha–style presentations (discussed in Chapter 3), composing and delivering "live-and-in-person" presentations add a level of vulnerability that is a bit different from writing a traditional text. In a written composition there is room for editing, revising, and peer review. In other words, writers are able to hide all of their work until they are comfortable sharing what they have composed. Even though composing presentations requires similar rhetorical moves such as structure, transitions, style, and voice, they inherently are live, spoken word engagements.

When presentations are given in Andy's classroom, he scores them and adds two things he genuinely enjoyed and one thing he wished, as an audience member, he would have seen. Then, after applauding the speaker's presentation, he meets them, rubric in hand, in the hallway for an immediate debriefing. As he and the speaker debrief in the hallway, the next speaker prepares for their own presentation.

It is in the hallway, away from the audience, where Andy chats with a student who has just finished their presentation. Conversations usually unfold in a manner similar to this:

The student stands by the wall fidgeting a bit. Andy smiles warmly, acknowledging the challenge of presenting, and says, "How did that feel?"

Student: *"Oh! I was just really nervous. I shouldn't have had so many words on each slide; I froze a couple of times, and it was just really bad."*

Andy: *"You were nervous? I didn't notice that at all. In fact, you seemed poised and confident."*

Student: *"Yeah, but . . ."*

Andy interrupts: *"Okay. Let's pause here for a second. It's too easy to beat yourself up and think about all the things you would like to do differently. Instead, let's focus on what you did well, and there are a lot of positives that came out of your presentation. What would you say are your 'pat-yourself-on-the-back moments'? The areas where you are proud of yourself?"*

Student: *"Okay, well, um, I thought my slides looked good and were easy to follow."*

Andy: *"Yes! They were beautiful! In fact, I commented on how the images you selected enhanced what you were saying. Look here,"* he points to a comment he wrote that echoes his sentiment, *"I said the same thing! They really were great. What else went right?"*

Student: Seeing that his self-reflection is similar to what Andy had thought, the student becomes more relaxed and says, *"I usually have note cards with me, but I wanted to try presenting without note cards this time, and I remembered everything I wanted to say."*

Andy: *"I love when that happens. When I present, my nerves surprise me every single time. I can't remember what I'm going to say and I'm afraid the presentation will flop. What would you say helped you not rely on note cards?"*

Student: *"I chose images that were relevant to what I was talking about. It really helped because I took my time and purposefully chose what to put where. It's like whenever I would get tripped up, I glanced at the images and they helped me remember what I wanted to say."*

Andy: *"I noticed that too, see?" he points to his comments. "And when you glanced up it triggered us audience members to look with you. You had us. We were invested, because you were invested."*

Student: *"Oh! I also reminded myself that this wasn't a presentation, that it was just an extended conversation like you talked to us about. That really helped."*

Andy: *"Right. It helps me, too. I'm proud of you. Here is how I scored your presentation." Andy discusses the grades. "You did great! Thanks for sharing your ideas with us." They shake hands and walk back into the classroom to watch the next presentation.*

Having the opportunity to pause, gather his thoughts, and debrief with Andy, this student was able to verbalize the positives of his presentation. It seemed clear to Andy that he left feeling affirmed because what he noticed matched what Andy had written. In other words, that move validated his positive comments, because Andy wasn't just giving him lip service; it was already written down before they began to chat.

Hallway debriefings catch students at a moment when they are already self-reflecting—a natural inclination. Taking advantage of the golden moment right after a presentation helps direct (or redirect) the energy students are using to think about how their presentation went. For students who already feel confident, the conversation serves as an affirmation seminar in which they receive praise as well as engage in thoughtful commentary. For students who do not feel confident, the conversation becomes a moment to focus on the positive. These are,

---

BOX 5.3: Formative Assessment

As they are finishing their essay, the presentation comes before the final draft is due. NCTE's *Professional Knowledge* reminds us that "[h]ow to assess students' work while they are in the process of writing—formatively—in order to offer timely assistance during the composing process" is an important skill for teachers to employ. In this case, with the hallway conversation, Andy was able to help this student move forward toward his final revisions.

perhaps, the most important moments, because a teacher's words have a powerful impact on how students view their ability as presenters. As Patty McGee concisely states about John Hattie's work: "Feedback is the heart and soul of strong instruction" (2017, p. 30). When students learn to view each situation they encounter as a growth moment, they experience areas of learning ready to be explored.

Grades (and Reasons to Stop Using Them)

As they write, inevitably one of our students asks one or all the following questions: "How long does this have to be?" "Is this for a grade?" "How many points is it worth?" or "Is there a rubric?" All of these are legitimate questions for students who are used to having every piece of writing evaluated; however, they are not questions for those who are interested in growing as writers.

In his book *Why They Can't Write*, John Warner laments that:

> . . . *many students hope college will be a fresh start after the grind of high school, but the legacy of stress and anxiety is difficult to escape. For so long, school has been about performance divorced from learning, so it's difficult to find value in anything other than an A. (p. 41)*

Having both taught college-level writers, we have seen this, too. And we wonder: How to determine what to focus on? What is the impact of our assessment? How do our assessment decisions encourage further writing growth?

Students are used to their writing being judged by others. But just because you are used to something does not mean it makes you feel any better about it.

We certainly don't feel any better about the noticeable shift from learning to grading that we encounter with our students. Still, we find ourselves in a system that—much to our dismay—focuses on a myopic letter grade that does not do much more than sort students into groups of "good" and "bad" writers. Implicit in this binary approach is a sense for students that, as writers, they were either born with the gift or they were not. In our view, writing is a continual process in which writers seek to push their own boundaries.

As writing teachers, we are called to do more with our students than simply ensure that they comply with our assignments. We are called to encourage the writers who walk through our door to explore, take risks, share, and grow their craft by taking our course. To accomplish this, we make an intentional shift in our

---

BOX 5.4: Assessment of Writing Involves Complex, Informed, Human Judgment

---

As NCTE has reiterated in policy statements and resolutions, including *Professional Knowledge*, "In order to provide high-quality writing opportunities for all students, teachers need to understand . . . how to assess occasionally, less frequently, in order to form and report judgments about the quality of student writing and learning." We continue to grow and change our own assessment practices as we also struggle to provide timely, specific feedback to our students, and this chapter outlines a number of ways we are assessing now.

---

thinking about the assessment of writing and, to deepen the conversation, what it means to write.

Stephen Tchudi writes, "[r]esponse to writing is, we believe, at the heart of the process" (1997). We are convinced that it is in our responses that teachers have the ability to become the gentle encouragers students need to combat the judge that rests in the mind of every writer. Yes, grades will come. But there is much work to do before those final marks arrive.

While we believe that feedback and a process of revision boost confidence in student writers, we also believe that the way we talk with students emboldens them to adopt a writer's identity. When students refer to themselves as writers and seek first the promising moves they make in a piece of writing, they are encouraged to risk more. The activities we share in this chapter are examples of feedback and revision protocols that build confidence in student writers.

Writing Activities that Encourage Feedback and Revision

With the activities described here, we show how our fifth principle of encouragement comes through our responses to feedback and revision; students are, indeed, mentor text explorers. We begin by inviting students to serve as authentic audiences and, subsequently, share examples that incorporate digital feedback and engage in conversations about revision with student questions about their work in mind.

ACTIVITY 5.1:

Empowering Students to Provide Substantive Feedback

Now that our writers have had a great deal of time to read, prewrite, and discuss their ideas, a critical phase begins: revision. And, in order to revise, writers need feedback. For students to earnestly receive feedback, a culture of support must be established; in her book *Peer Feedback in the Classroom* (2017), Starr Sackstein outlines the conditions necessary for students to give and receive effective feedback. She argues that:

> [d]eveloping a respectful classroom culture is not as easy as the warm and fuzzy sharing of experiences, although that is a fine start. Teachers need to safeguard student pride and ensure that the classroom is as free of negative judgment as possible. It isn't acceptable for students to say nasty things to one another or make fun of something they don't understand. It takes vigilance to make sure that all voices are being heard and respected in all classroom activities and situations. Respect can't be assumed; it must be taught explicitly and modeled continuously. Because students tend to follow our lead, the best way to elicit high-quality, respectful feedback is to start modeling these behaviors from day one. (pp. 19–20)

One way that Andy and Troy have found to help elicit these behaviors is through the use of protocols. In our own work as teacher-writers (Hicks, Busch-Grabmeyer, Hyler, & Smoker, 2013; Hicks et al., 2016; Schoenborn, 2014, 2018) and with our students, we have found many of the response protocols available through books like *The Power of Protocols: An Educator's Guide to Better Practice* (McDonald, Mohr, Dichter, & McDonald, 2013) and organizations like the National School Reform Faculty (2019) to be incredibly helpful.

One in particular, the Critical Friends Group protocol (National School Reform Faculty, 2017), is worth some exploration as it relates to Sackstein's point about creating respect in the writing classroom. As an additional

TABLE 5.1: Adaptation of the Critical Friends Protocol for Peer Response to Writing

		CRITICAL FRIENDS: COLLABORATING AS WRITERS	
Step	**Time**	**Peer Reviewers**	**Writer**
1	2–3 min	All writers come prepared to share; group selects first writer.	Once selected, the writer shares their work (in print or via Google Docs). Writer shares 2–3 main questions or concerns with the reviewers before reading begins.
2	3–5 min	Peer reviewers read the work, taking notes.	The writer composes an informal reflection about what they feels they did well.
3	3–5 min	Reviewers discuss: what parts of this piece move you as a reader? Peer reviewers talk to each other and offer warm feedback • engaging introductions • moments that pull the reader in • creative and strong analogies • effective and interesting transitions • powerful word choice/phrases	The writer listens silently, without entering into the conversation, and lists the warm feedback the peer reviewers discuss.
4	3–5 min	Peer reviewers talk to each other and offer cool feedback using conversation stems centered on the text. "As a reader, I . . ." • was confused when I read . . . • wish that . . . • appreciate when the writer said, "____" • wonder what might happen if . . . • found it difficult to read "_____," because . . ."	The writer listens silently, resisting the urge to enter the conversation, and takes notes on the cool feedback the peer reviewers discuss.

Step	Time	Peer Reviewers	Writer
5	3–5 min	After peer reviewers offer warm and cool feedback, the writer, who has refrained from commenting, is invited into the conversation to do the following: • Ask clarifying questions; • Agree with specific moments the peer reviewers noticed and explain why; • Disagree with specific moments the peer reviewers noticed and explain why; • Thank the peer reviewers for their feedback.	
6	1–2 min	Writers review their notes, naming their revision decisions, and then the group selects the next writer for response.	

Source: Adapted by Andrew Schoenborn from the National School Reform Faculty

resource for better understanding the Critical Friends protocol, we also encourage readers to view David Olio's video on the Teaching Channel (2014; linked from the chapter's page on the authors' website). The Critical Friends process allows a writer to listen in on how readers respond to their writing. It gives the writer an opportunity to zoom out of their text and prepare to make informed decisions as they revise their own work. The writer is not, however, the only beneficiary of the Critical Friends revision protocol. Examining texts in this way models and engages students as writers in collaboration with the aim to help everyone improve.

In his adaptation of this protocol, Andy puts students into groups of three. Each student comes prepared with their initial draft, and the group decides which student's work will be read and examined first. The student whose work is being examined remains silent, not part of the conversation and simply a notetaker, as a conversation around the student's text emerges from the other students in the group. While they do sometimes choose to print their writing and invite peers to comment in the margins, most often this peer response protocol has been conducted entirely through Google Docs. Table 5.1 describes the flow of conversation and the role each student plays during the revision protocol.

For Troy, the Critical Friends Protocol works a bit different. For his most recent freshman seminar, in which students were engaged in multimedia productions, he created a peer response form that, as partners, students would complete when nearly at the final stages of producing their projects. He provided a number of questions to help guide the conversation and, from the reviewer, he expected them to write a reflection on the peer response experience. He asked them to consider the following:

- To what extent do you feel the writer—in text, image, video, info-graphic, or other media—achieved one or more of these goals?
- In their writing (images, video, infographic, etc.), what has the writer demonstrated about issues related to social elements of digital culture?
- What evidence from the writer's work suggests that they have engaged in a substantive, iterative writing process?
- What suggestions did you offer to the writer to help move their work forward?
- Finally, as someone working on your own project, what specific writing strategies (textual or digital) did you notice in your peer's work that could be useful for you in your own work?

In this sense, Troy asks his students to use the opportunity for peer review as a kind of self-evaluation, too. This provides students with one final glimpse, through the lens of their peer's work, into their own writing process. A link to a template of this document can be found on this chapter's page on the authors' website.

During the Critical Friends protocol, or our adaptations, students tend to jump to what they want to change. To help resist the corrective urge, we explain to students that writing is, well, hard; the idea with a response such

---

BOX 5.5: Metacognition and Creativity

The Critical Friends protocol develops healthy metacognitive habits of mind, as noted in the *Framework*, when students "connect choices they have made in texts to audiences and purposes for which texts are intended." It is a strategy that compels students to apply the process of revision. Furthermore, the listening and reflecting done by writers during the Creative Friends protocol pushes and stretches their habit of creativity when they "evaluate the effects or consequences of their creative choices."

as this is to build their confidence while nudging them in fruitful directions. Using talk in this way is invaluable to a writer. They begin to literally hear what other readers think about a piece they have written. Knowing what piques your audience's interest, what confuses them, and what generates conversation removes the mystery of "what other people think" and encourages writers to carry on, dig in their heels, or reenvision the structure of a piece in insightful ways. As students master this skill in face-to-face conversations, we then invite them to move their work online.

ACTIVITY 5.2:
Enhancing Revision with Digital Feedback

We are well into the twenty-first century, and students find themselves writing in digital spaces daily. Teachers ask students to compose digitally more and more, though there are still questions about the overall effectiveness of keyboarding versus handwriting, at least as it pertains to notetaking and other basic writing tasks (Blair, 2015; Brundin, 2014; Chemin, 2014). Sidestepping that debate for the moment, we know that the digital is here to stay, and welcoming students to engage with us—and their peers—through a recursive process will most likely require digital writing tools at some point.

As we consider the ways in which we can provide feedback to students to help them revise—and the ways they can provide feedback to one another—it is of course worth noting that we do not use all of these tools all of the time, and that the strategic selection of particular tools depends on the writers, the task, and the timeline in which the response must be provided. For instance, in order to provide the most-timely feedback in as quick a manner as possible, we have found that recording a brief audio message ensuring that students hear our personal response is nearly as effective as conferring with them in person. However, as a draft enters its final stage and the revisions become more exacting, tracking changes and providing comments on the text itself can be more effective.

We acknowledge that when teachers are pressed for time, it can be easy to fall simply into corrective mode. Since we are interested in creating confident writers, we resist this urge. We both hold to the idea that, whatever new tools may be added, feedback on writing should focus first on global or higher-level concerns, or ideas related to the overall argument as well as the organization or themes of the writing. Then, a secondary focus is on local or lower-level concerns such as grammar and mechanics.

Before offering feedback on our students' writing—and when we ask students to read and respond to their peers—we do a full read of the writer's work before any comments are made. Then, as we notice patterns of errors or areas that need consideration, we identify those concerns as a reader would, noting positive, effective moments in the writing, too. Finally, we work to provide some ideas that will keep pushing writers forward in a productive manner, with aspirational goals. Writers need to know their words are read, appreciated, and contain hopeful moments if they are to become confident in their abilities. A useful approach for feedback, and one Andy shares explicitly with his students, includes the following:

- Start with a greeting.
- State the overarching ideas.
- Share two strengths of the piece.
- Share a large weakness of the piece.
- Add concluding remarks.

Approaching students' work in this way builds confidence in them as they begin to know what it means to be a writer. Jeff Anderson writes:

The knowing comes through the flow of student-teacher transactions, through students' observation . . . through students' talking, collecting, imitating, writing, experimenting, revising, editing, and reflecting. (2011, p. xiii)

Indeed, digital feedback increases the flow of interaction between students, peers, and teachers. There are a number of tools that we use to engage with writers, urging them to move toward revision. Though the technology is ever-changing, we offer a few ideas here for providing more effective feedback with digital tools (a list of links to these resources are available at this chapter's page on the authors' website).

As an example, let's pause for a moment to consider how student coauthors Hannah and Emma interact as they play with how to apply an archetypal lens to *King Lear*. Their feedback to each other spans the range of local and global, lower-level and higher-level concerns. A closer look reveals the following:

- Knowing the document will eventually be double-spaced in MLA form, Emma offers encouragement by saying, "Leave as single-space for now (that way the 4 pages or whatever is less intimidating :P) we can change it when we're done!" Emma's playful commentary is evident as she works to encourage her coauthor, which lightens the mood and also creates an energetic investment in a challenging piece.
- At another point of the piece, Hannah continues to play with ideas when she offers this notion: "CONCEPT: We scrap the whole 'biblical reference' idea and just focus on classic archetypes." Hannah and Emma are working through how they will synthesize what they learned about classical archetypes and modern interpretations. Ultimately, their view on those understandings reveal more about the characters in *King Lear*.
- A few days later, Hannah continues her playful tone and offers this suggestion: "OK LISTEN TO THIS ONE: We talk about the characters being examples of archetype XYZ then provide other examples of characters in literature that fit the bill i.e. Judas, Christ, Maleficent, Voldemort, Bilbo Baggins, Luke Skywalker, etc."

Hannah and Emma are writers who have developed a comfortable writing connection over the entire AP Literature class. They know themselves as writers, understand what works for them, and have found a productive banter that helps them grow. Of note, the comments are added in class, after school, and in the evening. Some of the best ideas for writers come when they least expect it, leading to substantive revision. Moreover, all of these interactions happened *before* the initial draft was submitted to Andy.

Once submitted to Andy by adding his email (and permission to edit) to the sharing settings, he reads the submitted piece and offers feedback, but withholds the grade until revisions are made and the document is submitted one final time. Allowing, and encouraging, the final resubmission, he adds, "Thank you for sharing. Please let me know when revisions are completed and I will score the piece." His comment encourages another check of the document by the authors and thus will become an easier piece to score during a second reading. Andy's move as a writing coach echoes Jeff Anderson's assertion that:

> *we can't motivate them to revise their writing by stapling a rubric or checklist to their paper. We can't motivate them by simply hanging some posters on the wall. We must facilitate writing behaviors. (2011, p. xiii)*

In our responses to students, we will also provide links to resources that can help them move forward with their writing. For instance, Andy pro-

---

BOX 5.6: Andy's Response to Emma and Hannah,
Providing Additional Resources and Links

Hello Emma and Hannah,
I LOVE the connections you've made between archetypes across the ages and genres. It demonstrates an interesting take and depth of thinking. The paper also does an admirable job of transitioning from idea to idea without losing the flow of the piece—hard to accomplish at times. I wonder, though, if you might sprinkle in some quotes to support your claims, attend to MLA form, and watch for paragraph breaks.

In my writing I have found these links useful:
MLA Format:
https://www.youtube.com/watch?v=iw0VmW-49ww

New-New Paragraph Technique:
https://www.teachwrite.org/single-post/2018/01/17/Paragraphs-Give-Us
-a-Break

Thank you for sharing. Please let me know when revisions are completed and I will score the piece.
I am excited to read more!

Mr. Schoenborn

vided the following summary to Hannah and Emma, being careful not to litter the document with too many comments (Box 5.6).

Another digital tool, the Chrome extension Draftback created by James Somers (link available on the authors' website), is available to teachers and students. The free extension offers objective process feedback based on curated revision history stamps found in every Google Doc. Using the embedded revision history stamps, Draftback creates a screencast of the entire writing process. As writers watch the letters, words, sentences, and paragraphs form, they can witness their process of writing as it unfolds over time. In addition, users are able to see the number of revisions they've made and the number of writing sessions they've engaged in (defined as periods where there wasn't more than a ten-minute gap between revisions); they can also view graphs of where they spent the most time on the document, as well as where their changes happened most frequently.

For example, Hannah and Emma spent a total of 5 hours and 34 minutes on the document. They were engaged in 1,322 distinct writing sessions during the process in which there wasn't more than ten minutes of inactivity. There was also a noticeable jump in writing activity after Andy offered his feedback, which indicates the effectiveness of his feedback to motivate

---

BOX 5.7: Persistence and Responsibility

It was this interaction that helped Hannah and Emma practice the successful postsecondary writing habit described by the *Framework* as persistence by "consistently tak[ing] advantage of in-class (peer and instructor responses) and out-of-class (writing or learning center support) opportunities to improve and refine their work." In addition, by Andy's choice to withhold a grade until they addressed the comments on his scale of concerns, Hannah and Emma demonstrated the habit of responsibility to "act on the understanding that learning is shared among the writer and others—students, instructors, and the institution, as well as those engaged in the questions and/or fields in which the writer is interested." Critical thinking was used to "read texts from multiple points of view (e.g., sympathetic to a writer's position and critical of it) and in ways that are appropriate to the academic discipline or other contexts where the texts are being used."

these writers. The information gathered from the Draftback extension becomes another real-time form of digital feedback that helps students better understand their writing process and build trust in that process.

As we continue to think about ways in which feedback and revision create confident writers, let's not forget that for students, submitting work they care about, like their Nerdy Book Club guest blog posts, is an authentic writing experience. But as soon as we add traditional rubrics, grades, or scores, that authentic experience that was worth aiming for becomes another writing exercise disguised in a mask of authenticity. When Andy asks his students to submit a piece of their writing for publication, he wants them to experience a process as close to the editorial review as possible. To accomplish this goal, he encourages students to revise and resubmit their chosen piece until both he and the writer(s) are satisfied.

ACTIVITY 5.3:
Revise and Resubmit

A cliché most everyone hears when they are younger is "we learn from our mistakes," and it is true. We do learn from our mistakes; but often, due to the pressures of time that we feel we need to cover the curriculum, students are not granted the time to take this sage advice. Instead, they are told to "try again next time" or that they "will have other opportunities in the future." Or they may make a few surface-level edits, but not truly engage in a meaningful revision process. The intent is well-meaning, but the reality is that, if students are not allowed to try again on the same assignment, they miss the chance to recalibrate the writing skills they are currently learning.

When authors submit a piece for publication, there is a standard anticipated by publishing editors who, as readers themselves, understand their audience. As the editors begin the peer-review process, there is a give-and-take of ideas that occurs to help tighten the piece. The choice of publication depends on many variables, but certainly the choices an author makes during the revision process, their response to criticism, and the reasoning for their rhetorical decisions, come into play. For the author, a revision review is a metacognitive exercise that builds confidence because the publishing editor is interested enough to explore the idea further.

One strategy that we have adapted from our own process of professional writing is the "revise and resubmit." The style may vary slightly depending on the assignment, but a "Revise and Resubmit Request" (or, in short, an "RRR") document will ask students to think purposefully about specific areas important to the task at hand. For instance, with the Nerdy Book Club submissions, once students have their initial feedback, they are asked to revise and submit an "RRR" that provides responses to the following:

- In what ways does your piece look similar to the mentor text you found on the Nerdy Book Club blog?
- In what ways does your piece include digital text features (e.g., links, images, subtitles, book covers, infographics, etc.)?
- In what ways does your piece respond to your trending topic?
- In what ways does your piece subtly incorporate the Book, Head, Heart framework?
- What other revisions have you made in order to anticipate and respond to readers' questions?

Without a mention of scores, grades, or scales of performance, students are able to focus on their choices as writers. Instead of attempting to reach

---

BOX 5.8: Openness and Creativity

In a similar fashion to publishing, students are encouraged to be open to feedback by engaging in what the *Framework* describes as "listen[ing] to and reflect[ing] on the ideas and responses of others—both peers and instructors—to their writing." When students are open to a process of receiving and responding to feedback, it generates creative opportunities as they "evaluate the effects or consequences of their creative choices." A process of revision is instrumental in developing rhetorical knowledge as students "write and analyze a variety of types of texts to identify the relationships among these key choices and the ways that the text(s) appeal or speak to different audiences."

the seemingly arbitrary expectations of a traditional rubric, students are immersed in authentic revision practices. These experiences build confidence in them over time as they come to know why and how their choices as a writer impact the reader while meeting a publisher's expectations.

Vulnerability is at the center of what it means to be a writer. It takes guts for a writer to tell their truth. It takes courage for a writer to leave no stone unturned. It takes a measure of fearlessness for a writer to share their work. The same is required of a writer when they receive feedback from readers. The writer knows what they want to say to their readers, but knowing what you want to say and articulating your ideas in a way you intend is an ever-present challenge for many writers.

Receiving feedback is no small task, either. Writers wonder: What will they think? How might their opinion of me change? What if they hate it? What if they love it? How will their feedback alter our relationship? If these are the kinds of questions you ask yourself, you understand the fortitude it takes to ask for and receive formative feedback.

Once a writer has feedback, it is up to them to decide what to do with it. This *is* the work of writing. It is a hurdle that many writers struggle to overcome. A process of writing invariably involves a cycle of overcoming self-doubt (however small), and when feedback is received it either confirms (and perpetuates) the writer's self-doubt or they choose to use it to learn, grow, and become stronger and more confident.

ACTIVITY 5.4:
Revising from Peer Response

As another form of multimodal composition, Troy's student Sarah Richmond and her classmates created a timeline specifically related to the history of transgender rights (a link to the timeline is on this chapter's page on the authors' website). Their inquiry for that particular pathway had begun with a question about a local school board and their vote to create gender-inclusive bathrooms in the fall of 2017. Several of the school board members were recalled through a special election, and Sarah's group decided that it would be interesting to explore the issue and reach out to the newspaper reporter who had been covering the case. In their expert interview, the reporter gave Sarah and her team even more ideas to build from.

With fifteen separate events on their timeline, Sarah's group wrote entries from at least a few sentences all the way up to full paragraphs about each of the events, providing context as well as an appropriate image to represent the event. Having begun their inquiry with just a few ideas about how transgender rights and related stories were playing out in the news, Sarah and her classmates decided to use another of Knight Lab's tools, Timeline JS. While the nature of online communication can sometimes be described as pithy, and Sarah's group thought that an image in a simple explanation for each was enough, they ended up producing a multimodal project that included writing of just over 1,000 words, beyond the expectation of the assignment and complete with images to represent each of these moments. More importantly, they documented their sources in an addendum and included appropriate hyperlinks on the timeline itself.

For instance, as it related to the school board controversy, Sarah and her classmates summarized the issue as well as individual board members' record of voting. Then they reviewed the crux of the case on one of the timeline entries, noting the community response. The community is still feeling the effects of the controversy as—at the time of this writing—local journalists are still reporting on the lingering effects of the policy implementation and the recall election. In addition to summarizing the case, Sarah and her classmates also provided links to a recent article filed by the reporter to whom they had spoken, citing their own source in both a direct and academically appropriate manner.

For Sarah, the peer review process was particularly helpful. She noted in her course reflection: "The last peer review that I did actually really helped my final project on divulging into the history of transgender issues, as my peer reviewer actually gave me an idea on what I should add to give more valuable and useful information to the timeline my group and I were making." In the end, Sarah and her classmates were able to respond to the needs of their audience, while still balancing the need for clear and concise information with the many affordances of multimedia.

Conclusion

Revision is perhaps the trickiest part of a writing process. It is the time when a writer really learns what they had to say on a given topic. There will always be moments to celebrate within a piece; writers should celebrate those moments, as they are what keep us coming back to the page. Writers also know there will be work to be done. As writing teachers, if we can keep our students centered on what they are doing well, we will increase their motivation to see the work through.

Consider your own stance on revision, as well as what it means to move writers toward revision. After reading the chapter, being introduced to ideas about feedback and encouraging revision, we invite you to write, talk, and think about the following:

- In what ways do we invite and encourage students to engage in a substantive revision process, without the fear of grades attached to it?
- What elements of the author's craft—in both print text and digital writing—are worth our students' time and energy as they revise?
- How can we build structured means of response via protocols, both face-to-face and online?
- Over an entire unit or semester, what is a reasonable amount of revision to expect, and with which assignments should we require (as compared to suggest) these revisions?

CELEBRATE

CHAPTER 6

Reflection and Celebrating Growth

"'I am not a writer' is a phrase I would often tell myself, and when you say something so often, it is not hard to start believing it. This class shifted my definition of what a writer truly is—for me it is someone who enjoys to write—I am a writer and I enjoy writing."

—Ryan Backus, MPHS

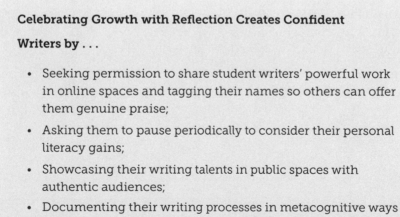

Celebrating Growth with Reflection Creates Confident Writers by . . .

- Seeking permission to share student writers' powerful work in online spaces and tagging their names so others can offer them genuine praise;
- Asking them to pause periodically to consider their personal literacy gains;
- Showcasing their writing talents in public spaces with authentic audiences;
- Documenting their writing processes in metacognitive ways that create a visible account of their growth as writers.

Writers need to see where they've been, both to reflect on what's worked well and to celebrate their growth.

In any writing workshop (or project-based learning environment), there comes a moment when the window through which students have been viewing their project comes to a close. A project has been in process, perhaps for a few days or even for many weeks. At that moment, it is tempting for everyone to close the window and move on to the next of many tasks.

However, if decades of research on education and psychology have taught us anything, we need to wonder: What if we lingered in the learning for just a bit? What would we say about our experience? Where have we grown? How did we meet our own expectations as well as the expectations of the assignment?

It is in these moments when windows close that students can begin to notice what changes, seeing how the boundaries of what they have learned continue to expand. A grade alone doesn't really tell students or teachers what was learned in class, and moving students toward a more substantive reflection is difficult. But it is worth the challenge.

An intentional process of reflection "transforms a student's action in the classroom from the empty satisfying of a teacher's assignments to a real learning experience that . . . builds something lasting for the writer" (Whitney, McCracken, & Washell, 2019, p. 2). One of the lasting experiences we hope our students walk away with is that they no longer feel the need to rely on extrinsic motivation like points, grades, and rubrics, and instead on the intrinsic sense of satisfaction that writing can produce when goals are conceived, carried out, met, and celebrated. To a writer, that is all the motivation they need to write.

A writer's process is, as Kathleen Blake Yancy reminds us, informed by reflection: "as they learn, they witness their own learning: they show us how they learn" (1998, p. 8). There is opportunity for us, as teacher-writers, to point toward celebratory moments we see in a student's writing that they may not see themselves. When we witness a student overcome fear or self-doubt, celebrate. When their risk to write in an unfamiliar genre is met with success, celebrate. When they write for just a bit longer, when they trust themselves enough to reenvision a piece, and when they are brave enough to push the submit button and go public, celebrate and cheer them on. Writing is hard—and writers can use all the support we can give.

As a mentor in your own classroom, inviting, encouraging, and celebrating writing are all critical to build the confidence within your students to write. In the first two chapters we narrowed our focus on writing invitations in the spaces we create and how those spaces lead to student writing goals. In the next three chapters we turned our attention to practices that encourage writing and how they move writers forward.

We pivot here, once again, to focus on moments worthy of reflection and

---

BOX 6.1: Connection to Professional Knowledge

As noted in many places throughout the *Framework* and *Professional Knowledge* documents, reflection is a critical component of the writing process. The *Professional Knowledge* statement in particular notes that "[i]n order to provide high-quality writing opportunities for all students, teachers need to understand . . . ways people use writing for personal growth, expression, and reflection, and how to encourage and develop this kind of writing." In this spirit, we see writing for reflection as equally as important as writing to summarize, synthesize, or argue.

---

celebration that create confidence and solidify writerly identities in the minds of students. Reflection is how a writer comes to understand what pulls them to the page or the screen. Celebration is the experience that keeps a writer coming back. It is through these acts of self-discovery that "turn experience into learning" and reinforce their belief that they are, indeed, writers (Boud, Keogh, & Walker, 1985, p. 19).

We encourage you to join us in collegial conversation about approaches to writing, this time focused on reflecting on and celebrating student growth. When teaching writing, we consider these questions:

- Through the conversations we conduct, do we encourage our students to reflect on their writing processes by asking them to acknowledge the moments in which they shine?
- Through the assignments we create, do we offer intentional moments for students to pause, reflect, and write about the ways in which they are growing as writers?
- By introducing students to digital curation spaces like blogs, do we create portfolios of student work for them to revisit at the end of a trimester or semester?
- Over the course of a trimester or semester, do we seek permission to showcase their work in public and digital spaces with targeted audiences in mind?

Portfolios as Portraits of Growth

By the time Andy's students reach his classes in high school, students have had over a decade's worth of experience in a school setting. Each year students start afresh with a teacher they (most likely) have not learned from before, and for many students a new English teacher means a varied pedagogical approach. It follows that each experience requires students to adjust to meet the expectations of the class. A student's educational journey has many, many variables they negotiate through the years. Yet, there is one constant that remains regardless of who they have for a teacher: themselves. They are present in the class.

Regardless of educational experience, a student has the ability to choose how they interact with their classes. With that in mind, students need to learn to trust themselves, the decisions they make as readers and writers, and *why* they make the choices they do if they are to become confident as literate adults, especially so as confident writers.

Think back on your literacy journey for a moment. If it was anything like ours, there were moments of great leaps of learning and rich experiences; there were moments of plateaus; and there were, though we hate to admit it, valleys in which we carried on. The totality of those moments and how we chose to respond to them shaped our view of literacy. They shape our students' view of literacy as well.

Common sense seems to say that on the first day of school, we need to build relationships with students by using icebreakers as well as share overviews of the course by reviewing the syllabus. In lieu of the typical icebreaker and syllabus review, Andy distributes a digital permission form (available on the authors' website) for students and caretakers to sign, and he uses the first few days of a trimester to explain and introduce Edublogs as the platform they will use to curate their reflections on literacy processes.

The topics and timings of each post thus match natural reflective moments within a trimester. The "Living Your Literacy Journey" post sets the stage by taking advantage of each student's sense of a new start at the beginning of a trimester. At the midpoint and the final week of a trimester, students polish a choice creative writing piece of their choice, analyze their reading habits, and reflect on their newly finished project. These reflective posts culminate in a reflective final exam that ties all of the ideas together. The reflective final exams, detailed in Activity 6.3, bring a trimester-long course full circle and refocus students on their growth, effort, risk-taking, and assessment of themselves as literate people.

Looping posts focused on process reflection asks students to pause and take a

Process Posts	Post Topics	Post Details	Trimester (12 weeks)
	TABLE 6.1: Reflective Blog Posts Looped Throughout a Trimester		
Blog post 1	Living Your Literacy Journey	Activity 2.1	Week 1
Blog post 2	Publishable Choice Creative Writing Piece 1	Activity 1.1	Week 6
Blog post 3	Independent Reading Analysis 1	Activity 6.1	Week 6
Blog post 4	Growth Territories	Activity 6.2	Week 6
Blog post 5	Publishable Choice Creative Writing Piece 2	Activity 1.1	Week 11
Blog post 6	Independent Reading Analysis 2	Activity 6.1	Week 11
Blog post 7	Growth Territories	Activity 6.2	Week 11
Blog post 8	Reflective Final Exam	Activity 6.3	Week 12

pulse of their literacy progression threaded throughout the course. Table 6.1 gives a bird's-eye view of where the reflective process posts fall in a twelve-week trimester. You can, of course, adjust each post to fit the needs of your district's trimester or semester calendar.

Though each assigned blog post has been detailed throughout the book, we think it is important to focus on how Andy uses these posts to build confident writers as he balances their growth with grades. What follows are the promising practices of metacognitive reflection as a series of blog posts during a trimester.

Living Your Literacy Journey: Reflecting on Goal-Oriented Identities

For each reflective blog post, Andy creates an open workshop structure for students to effectively consider their literacy goals during the week before finals. Their first blog post addresses four metacognitive literacy talking points that address critical questions for goal-oriented identities. See Table 6.2, as well as the authors' website, for additional links to these surveys and a sample student text.

Students share their journey as a way to lead into their literacy identities. Then, using a reading survey, students share who they are currently as readers. Next, students shift their focus to considering writing identities by using a writing survey. After considering where they have been with the journey and where they are now

TABLE 6.2: Blog Post #1: Living Your Literacy Journey

Blog Post #1: Living Your Literacy Journey – Week 1

Blog Post #1 Expectations	Goal-Oriented Identities: Critical Questions

Living Your Literacy Journey
 	
   + Reading survey
 	
   + Writing survey
 	
   + Literacy goals
 	
   = Student mentor text
	Literacy experiences:
	• Where have I been? What are my literacy roots? What are my literacy branches?
	• What does your current reading/writing life look like?
	• What are the ways in which you read/write on your own? How does this compare with reading/writing in school?
	• How would you describe your relationship with reading/writing? Are you currently "in a relationship"? "seeking a relationship"? "on again, off again"? or "not interested"? Share your reasoning.
	• What keeps your relationship with reading alive? What are you looking for in a reading relationship? What pushes you away from reading?
	
	Challenges and Sparks – Reading/Writing:
	• Who am I as a reader? Who am I as a writer?
	• What are the challenges, both small and significant, that have affected your abilities and confidence as a reader? As a writer?
	• What have been your challenges with reading? With writing?
	• What topics, genres, and authors excite you as a reader? As a writer?
	• What are your passions, interests, and deeply held beliefs about how you learn best as a reader? As a writer?
	• Recall and reflect on your reading sparks: What pulls you into reading?
	• How might what you read impact how/what you write?
	• Recall and reflect on your writing sparks: What pulls you into writing?
	• How might what you write impact how/what you read?
	
	Literacy Goals:
	• Where do I want to be?
	• What are three to four reading and writing goals you have for the trimester?
	• How many books do you plan on reading?
	• Are you interested in writing for real audiences?
	• Have you considered a form of publication, whether it be small or significant?
	• What habits of mind might you need to accomplish these goals?

as readers and writers, students write with a mind to the future. They share three to four goals as readers, writers, and critical thinkers.

Crafting Confidence:
Reflecting on Writer-Oriented Identities

In the second and fifth blog posts, students address two metacognitive creative writing talking points that address critical questions for writer-oriented identities. See Table 6.3 for more details on these.

The process for independent creative writing posts is detailed in Activity 1.1, but the focus is on helping students build an identity as a writer. Students share a publishable creative writing piece in order to see it to its conclusion and to step outside of their comfort zone as they build confident writing identities. Although his students may submit any genre of creative writing they wish, Andy often encourages students to submit poetry because there is more room for playful interaction, less focus on formal rules of writing, and an opportunity to share powerful pieces.

Then, students use revision tips and strategies to sift for gold as they seek power found in their own words. Next, adapted from Amy Ludwig VanDerwater's work, *Poems Are Teachers*, students share "words from the author" in which they discuss their inspiration for the piece. Lastly, inspired by Jeff Anderson and Deborah Dean's work, *Revision Decisions*, students reflect on the one significant revision decision they made and why it was a turning point in the piece.

Certainly, during this process some pieces shine a little brighter than others

TABLE 6.3: Blog Posts #2 and #5: Publishable Choice Creative Writing	
Blog Posts #2 and #5: Publishable Choice Creative Writing - Weeks 6 and 11	
Blog Post #2 and #5 Expectations	**Writer-Oriented Identities: Critical Questions**
HD summative image (Pixabay or Unsplash) + Revise/edit creative piece + Words from the author + Revision decision = Student mentor text	**Words from the author:** • Why did you choose this piece? • Where is a place that holds energy or emotion? • Where did the idea come from? **Revision decision:** • What was a specific revision you made that added power? • What was your inspiration?

and, for those pieces, Andy invites students to publish them on his LiveWrite web page. He uses these as examples of student-created mentor texts as well as a showcase to celebrate student words and to build confidence.

Reading Strides: Reflecting on Reader-Oriented Identities

In the third and sixth blog posts, students address one metacognitive reading analysis talking point that addresses critical questions for reader-oriented identities. See Table 6.4 for more details.

TABLE 6.4: Blog Posts #3 and #6: Independent Reading Analysis	
Blog Posts #3 and #6: Independent Reading Analysis – Weeks 6 and 11	
Blog Post #3 and #6 Expectations	**Reader-Oriented Identities: Critical Questions**
HD self-taken picture of books read + Marking period X reading analysis + Paragraph form = Student mentor text	**Volume and stamina:** • Total pages read this marking period = _____ • Pages per week average = _____ • Is this more than usual? If so, why? If not, why not? • Estimate your growth in stamina. • How long can you read at once? • Has this changed this marking period? **Independent reading selections:** • What did you read (genres, authors) this marking period? • What did you love? **Independent reading habits:** • Where and when do you get most of your reading done? (include both home and school reading) • What is your goal for the total number of books you can read this trimester? • This school year? **Summary:** • What have you learned about yourself as a reader this marking period? • How do you plan to challenge yourself as a reader during the next marking period?

The process for independent reading analysis posts is detailed in Activity 6.2, and the focus is on helping students build an identity as a reader. Adapted from Penny Kittle's reading analysis work in *Book Love*, this post serves as a look in the mirror for students to consider how they are establishing positive reading habits and routines. Andy stresses the importance of building relationships with books of their choice. When students find themselves interested in maintaining those relationships with books, they increase their likelihood of choosing to read outside of the classroom. These posts are meant to be quick self-evaluative check-ins to see that their relationships with books are progressing.

Growth Territories: Reflecting on Learner-Oriented Identities

In the fourth and seventh blog posts, students address three learning territories that address critical questions for growth-oriented identities. See Table 6.5 for more.

The process for the growth territories post is detailed in Activity 6.2 with a focus on helping students explore a growth mindset. As teachers, we certainly have a plan for student learning targets, but learning isn't so straightforward; it pro-

TABLE 6.5: Blog Posts #4 and #7: Growth Territories

Blog Posts #4 and #7: Growth Territories - Weeks 6 and 11

Blog Post #4 and #7 Expectations	Learner-Oriented Identities: Critical Questions
HD summative image (Pixabay or Unsplash) + Growth territories + 3–5 areas of growth + 1 standard met for each growth area + 1 screenshot for most significant growth area = Student mentor text	**Metacognitive Talking Points:** • Where have you stepped outside of your comfort zone? • How have you nudged at the edges of your understanding? • What felt risky at one time, but does not feel that way anymore? • What was your most significant growth area? • Why do you believe you experienced growth?

gresses in an ebb and flow of experiences that grow for each student at different rates. If teachers are interested in knowing how their students have grown over the course of a unit, we are better served by asking them ourselves. Still, students tend to have a fixed mindset when it comes to learning. For most students to have learned something means an epiphany or a paradigm shift they were not expecting, and, yes, while those are certainly learning gains that are easily identifiable, most learning does not happen that way.

Instead of a sudden change in perspective, a process of learning usually occurs slowly, at the edges of a student's understanding. As students take new steps outside of their comfort zones it can feel risky, but once they become comfortable the sense of risk they once felt diminishes. Growth territory posts ask students to look in the rearview mirror and consider those anxious moments that now feel a bit more comfortable. While we, as teachers, understand that an increase in comfort levels indicates growth and learning, it is more difficult for students to recognize it unless they are asked to reflect on their growth.

Reflective Final Exam: Reflecting on a Trimester of Progress

In the eighth blog post, students take a long view of their learning that addresses critical questions for learner-oriented identities. See Table 6.6 for more details.

The process for the reflective final exam post is detailed in Activity 6.3 with a focus on helping students consider the goals they set for themselves and how well they were able to meet those goals. The reflective nature of these exams takes advantage of the natural inclination people have when they are nearing the end of a course. What might normally be quick thoughts for students about how they did in a class has now become a richer introspection—one that brings a course gently to a close as it prompts students to consider what the future holds for them.

Choosing how we assess students and their writing plays a critical role in giving lift to writing identities. In each reflective blog post, Andy situates his students in a space that asks them to consider their role in a process of learning. The message is clear: progress is more important than perfection.

Each of the blogfolio checkpoints takes advantage of what we noted earlier in Chapter 2. Daniel Pink calls this the "fresh start effect" (2018, p. 95). Whenever people are on the cusp of something new, like beginning a class or starting a new project, personal temporal landmarks emerge in the mind's eye. Whether a "preflection" or metacognitive reflections at checkpoints during a trimester, personal

TABLE 6.6: Blog Post #8: Reflective Final Exam

Blog Post #8: Reflective Final Exam - Week 12

Blog Post #8 Expectations	Learner-Oriented Identities: Critical Questions
HD summative image (Pixabay or Unsplash) + Reflective final exam + Goals, effort, intellectual risk-taking, growth, effort, and self-assessment + Blogfolio evidence = Student mentor text	**Goals:** • Why did you choose the goals you wrote about in your "Future Me" letter? Did you meet those goals? Why or why not? **Effort:** • Where did you put the most effort? What did you notice about the impact it had on that learning goal? **Intellectual Risk-Taking:** • Which intellectual risk seemed to have the richest reward? How did it shift your approach? **Growth:** • Upon review of your blogfolio, which moments stand out as significant growth? **Self-Assessment** • Why do you believe you are adding to your overall literacy repertoire?

temporal landmarks serve two purposes. First, as Pink argues, they "allow people to open 'new mental accounts,'" offering a chance to start again (p. 95). Second, they "shake us out of the tree so we can glimpse the forest—causing people to take a big picture view of their lives and thus focus on achieving their goals" (p. 96). In the sometimes-hectic nature of new learning that takes place in a course, these "temporal landmarks slow our thinking, allowing us to deliberate at a higher level and make better decisions" (p. 96). For literacy growth and especially writing, these landmarks build confidence in students as they see, for themselves, a literacy momentum moving in a positive direction.

For Troy, reflections happen at the end of each of three major projects and again in the final essay and presentation of the semester. At the end of these projects, he invites students to share a brief reflection in writing and via Flipgrid, a video-based discussion forum that was recently purchased by Microsoft and made available to any educator for free use. With the ability to set up threaded topics and with the duration of video responses from just a few seconds to a few minutes, Flipgrid offers writing teachers a unique space for their students to share their reflections and engage with their peers.

For instance, at the end of the Digital ID project, outlined in Chapter 1, Troy asked students to respond in a brief, 3-minute video to the following prompt:

- Now that you have wrapped up your own digital ID—and viewed the work of your classmates—consider the following:
  — What have you learned about yourself as a writer? In what ways have you been creative, flexible, and persistent?
  — What have you learned about yourself as a digital author? How has "creating to learn" worked for you?
  — Finally, what have you learned about yourself and the many identities that you bring with you to college? What resonates most? What will you carry forward?

In the responses to this set of questions, students needed to be succinct yet still thoughtful. As they discussed the various aspects of their writing process and their use of digital tools, they were able to reflect candidly on the successes achieved and what the process of "creating to learn" (Hobbs, 2017) meant for them. Hearing them articulate these ideas, Troy was then able to offer even more feedback about their writing process, encouraging them to move ahead with the knowledge and skills they had gained as they began their next project.

BOX 6.2: Assessment of Writing Involves Complex, Informed, Human Judgment

While we understand that there are times and places in which numerical scores, even scores generated through automated assessment of writing, can be useful, both Andy and Troy steer away from rubrics and computerized analysis of student work. Instead, we both agree with NCTE 's Professional Knowledge in that "[i]n order to provide high-quality writing opportunities for all students, teachers need to understand . . . how to use portfolios to assist writers in their development and how to assess portfolios." In the end, we believe that the use of portfolios offers a more nuanced and complete portrait of the writers we serve.

Writing as communication is a critical component for learning, growing, and gaining access to the positions that students are seeking. Words are powerful, and the way students choose to craft their thoughts will either create opportunities or become a barrier to their success. What is at stake is our students' livelihood— their ability to make their mark on the world—and becoming confident in their ability to communicate effectively will break down barriers.

Branching Out: Moving Celebrations Out of the Classroom

It is one thing to celebrate the work of student writers in the classroom. However, many writers may begin to wonder if the praise they receive is warranted or if it is nothing more than a kind gesture. Although genuine praise is affirming inside the walls of the classroom, and certainly builds confidence, there comes a time when every writer is ready to spread their wings.

Still, for many, sharing their work is intimidating at best or paralyzing at worst, and writers could use a gentle nudge. On occasion, a piece of student writing is so well crafted it simply needs to be shared with the world. When this happens, Andy takes a moment to chat with the student. He compliments their work, then with specific reasoning describes what he admires about it, and finally asks permission to share their work online. Not wanting to put too much pressure on any student, he assures them that it is okay to decline the invitation to go public.

Rarely do students decline Andy's invitation. To a writer, there is nothing that builds confidence more than to know someone values their work so much that they want to tell others about it. If the student grants permission, Andy adds it to the collection of student poetry on his LiveWrite blog. Then he asks if they have a Twitter handle and, if so, posts their work online, tagging students themselves and members of professional organizations, seeking comments for the students' work. Although it's possible for students to receive negative comments, it rarely happens. On the off-chance that the student receives negative comments, Andy and the student consider those remarks through the lens of a writer. By targeting and tagging respected organizations like @NCTE, @writingproject, and @ILAToday, student poets soak in all the love from real audiences far and wide.

Positive feedback is worth celebrating in the classroom, and Andy makes it a point to show the subsequent tweet thread with the class at the beginning of the next class period. This recognition gives the writer another celebratory moment, this time with peer recognition and snaps all around for the showcased work.

Sharing student poetry online is one step that creates confidence in writers.

BOX 6.3: Assessment of Writing Involves Complex, Informed, Human Judgment

Again, assessments do not always need to be tied to grades, and they can also be generative spaces for students to share their ideas with others. As NCTE notes in Professional Knowledge, "In order to provide high-quality writing opportunities for all students, teachers need to understand . . . the uses of writing in public presentations and the values of students making oral presentations that grow out of and use their writing." Andy's collaboration with Art Reach is one example of how his students can engage in an authentic display of their work for an audience of their peers and community members.

After a couple of trimesters, however, the amount of talented poetry produced needs outlets beyond what online spaces can provide. So, partnering with his local community arts center, Art Reach, Andy organizes a spoken word event he calls "Youth Voices Rising." The event features talented writers who were encouraged to perform their work and have also accepted the invitation.

The Art Reach Center helps to advertise the event, offers space at no cost for students to perform, and on the evening of the event, contains an audience of community members, family, and friends. It is a tremendous celebration of language, talent, work, and writing. Students walk away understanding that their words matter and feel pride knowing their voices were heard. Moments like these are a gift for writers that no amount of classroom snaps can equal. We encourage you to look for spaces outside of your classroom, either online, in public, or both, to celebrate student writing.

Suffice it to say, when teachers structure in-class time for purposeful reflection, students who enter fully into the process grow as writers. By incorporating reflective routines, teachers reinforce the habits of mind found in the framework for postsecondary success. Moreover, teachers who seek opportunities to celebrate the successes of student writing, both inside and outside of the classroom, will see student confidence grow as they take more risks, share more work, and seek more opportunities to go public.

Writing Activities that Help Students Reflect on Growth

We now present three additional activities that help students reflect on their growth and also provide us with opportunities to celebrate their success. With the "Reading Analysis Blog Post" outlined in Activity 6.1, a more explicit connection is made to the texts students have been exploring. Then, in Activity 6.2, the "Growth Territories Blog Post," Andy has students create two of these similar posts in a 12-week trimester—though this version is focused on what he asks them to do at the end of the Shakespearean drama project. Finally, with Activity 6.3, we can see how students' earlier reflections can accumulate in a final exam and reflective essay for Andy's course.

ACTIVITY 6.1:
Reading Analysis Blog Post

As noted in Chapter 4, it is possible to become a reader without writing, but the chances of becoming a writer without reading are slim. Given the work that he asks them to do as readers, Andy's students have a variety of artifacts from which they can draw as they prepare to create two reading analysis blog posts, one at the midpoint of the trimester and another at the end. Building off a strategy described by Penny Kittle in *Book Love*, Andy invites students to create realistic challenges and set weekly goals. Kittle describes it in the following manner:

> *During the first week of class, I ask students to find a book they would like to read and to read silently, at a comfortable pace, for 10 minutes . . . The goal is understanding, not speed . . . at the end of 10 minutes each student records the number of pages read in that time . . . what I'm trying to establish is a measure to make the homework reading I'm going to assign fair to all. (p. 27)*

This rate of reading becomes a baseline by which students can track their progress, and it encourages them to make choices and set goals (rather than having a "personalized" learning program that measures their reading levels do it for them). Reading analysis opens up conversations between writers that may not happen otherwise. Though writers may not keep an analysis of this type for their own reading lives, students need to develop healthy reading habits, and the reading analysis helps them to make the reading/writing connection. Writers who know themselves as readers are writers better suited to connect with their audience.

In preparation for writing their blog post, Andy asks students to answer the following questions as a form of prewriting:

- Volume and stamina
  — Total pages read this marking period: _____
  — Pages per week average: _____
  — Is this more than usual? If so, why? If not, why not?
  — Estimate your growth in stamina. How long can you read at once? Has this changed during this marking period?
- Reading selections
  — What did you read (genres, authors) this marking period?
  — What did you love?
- Reading habits
  — Where and when do you get most of your reading done? (Please include both home and school reading.)
  — What is your goal for the total number of books you can read this trimester? This school year?
- Summary
  — What have you learned about yourself as a reader this marking period?
  — How do you plan to challenge yourself as a reader during the next marking period?

Given the goal of creating confident writers, inviting students to set and reach reading goals keeps them in conversation with books, exposing them to many writing voices, some of which they may choose to try on in their own writing. Consider twelfth-grade student Tori Davis's refreshing take on her reading experience (Davis, 2018). She read three books related to her personal interest in women's studies: *Asking for It* (O'Neill, 2016), *Written on the Body* (Winterson, 1993), and *Oranges Are Not the Only Fruit* (Winterson, 1997).

BOX 6.4: Metacognition and Engagement

A reflective analysis of her independent reading choices helped Tori enter into a metacognitive process, as described by the *Framework*, to "use what [she] learn[ed] from reflections on one writing project to improve writing on subsequent projects." Through her reflection she found it engaging to "make connections between [her] own ideas and those of others." While reflecting on her reading, Tori was also developing knowledge of conventions to "read and analyze print . . . texts composed in various styles, tones, and levels of formality."

By reading these stories I found that they helped me grow so much as a reader and even as a writer, I discovered more within myself and my own love for reading which had simmered out over the years . . . I would say I also grew as a reader because of these novels which gave me a more challenging read and forced me to read deeper into these stories.

In her response she is recognizing the impact of choice reading and writing as she develops a positive inner voice critical to her growing confidence, a voice that moves her toward writing. Her full response is linked from this chapter's page on the authors' website.

ACTIVITY 6.2:
Growth Territories Blog Post

At the end of their unit on Shakespearean drama, Andy provides students with an opportunity to take stock of their learning by identifying three to five significant growth territories within the broad categories of reading, writing, and thinking. He reintroduces students to *The Framework for Success in Postsecondary Writing* so they can use some of the habits of mind as a way to identify key aspects of their learning, and he also asks them to include an image that, metaphorically, represents all they have learned.

With the Shakespeare unit, students have a variety of individual activities and broader themes on which they can focus:

- The choice of a particular drama, as well as the critical theory through which they analyzed that drama;
- The process of viewing the drama in film, watching it once to get a general sense of the story and a second time to conduct a deeper analysis;
- Critical theory conversations with their classmates as well as a visit from a university professor who is a Shakespearean scholar;
- The process of writing itself, with specific attention to developing a thesis/focus for the research paper and using MLA style;
- The process of creating and delivering a final presentation, discussing intentional choices made by the team;
- The experience, as a viewer and listener, when watching classmates deliver their presentations;
- Any other moments in the unit including "aha" experiences while reading, conferring with Mr. Schoenborn, or significant takeaways from class discussions.

He ends the assignment with this encouragement: "Please remember to keep your posts positive to encourage a growth mindset!"

Esme, whom we first met in Chapter 2, offers compelling insight as she reflects on growth territories while immersed in her Shakespearean drama project. The first area of growth, choosing her critical literary theory and doing subsequent research about it, led to a realization that occurred only through the process of writing. She describes her first territory as the use of critical theory:

> If I'm being completely honest here, I told everyone that I knew exactly what I was going to write my paper on but, the truth is, I didn't know where to start or even what existentialism was . . . [I] was suddenly more excited to be doing my paper on something as in depth as the moral and thought processes of fictional characters

from one of the most famous playwrights in history . . . Due to all of these things that I figured out along the way, I feel as if I've grown the most here [with my use of critical theory].

Through her reflection, Esme reveals that although she presented a confident stance as a writer, it wasn't until she dove into a topic that interested her—existentialism—that she became more excited about her work on the project. She was offered choice and flexibility in approaching a challenging project that afforded her latitude to find her entry point into a literary theory she found compelling.

In another growth territory, Esme acknowledges the power of conferencing to build a writer's confidence before diving into the deep end of complex piece of writing. Talking through an approach to a piece of writing with another experienced writer many times affirms and, subsequently, builds her confidence as a writer to be bold:

While I didn't come up with my actual topic until I was on my own, the debriefing helped me out a lot. I think that the most helpful thing was speaking about my theory proposal. Mr. Schoenborn really did go through, read my proposal, and thoroughly explained what he liked and thought I could improve on for my paper. He also added a few of his experiences in, as well, which helped me to focus more on the task at hand.

In making this comment, Esme recognizes the value of conferencing with teachers who can share ideas, writer to writer, in a genuine conversation about their plan of attack on a piece of writing. She is, once again, making concrete the benefits of conferring with others who are interested in helping her achieve her writing goals. In these reflections, centered on specific growth territories, Esme reveals her process of writing, which is a measure of growth no standardized test is able to articulate with adequate precision. As teachers, we begin to learn who our students are as writers along with them as they each stretch their writer's identity in ways they might not recognize had they not paused to reflect on their process.

By being intentional in the act of thinking about her process, Esme and her classmates stand a greater chance of not simply moving on to whatever next project, task, or unit the teacher has planned—the next stop on the conveyor-belt tour of education that leads to a diploma. We agree with John Hattie who, in his book *Visible Learning for Teachers: Maximizing Impact on Learning* (2011), insists that:

> the aim is to get the students actively involved in seeking this evidence: their role is not simply to do tasks as decided by teachers, but to actively manage and understand their learning gains. This includes evaluating their own progress, being more responsible for their learning, and being involved with peers in learning together about gains in learning. (p. 88)

Yes, it takes classroom time for Andy to engage students in this metacognitive approach to verbalizing their personal learning growths. However, these moments produce realizations for student writers that no teacher can teach: the realization that they are learning and growing in unexpected ways, and that writing can bring intellectual joy, if we let it.

Writing and reflecting on growth territories once every six weeks is a piece of a larger picture of growth over time. It is a component in an ever-expanding body of evidence of personal learning contained within a blog portfolio. The responses students leave help Andy to consider what is working and what is not in his writing instruction. He adjusts his

---

BOX 6.5: Metacognition and Responsibility

Reflecting, in writing, on her areas of growth helped Esme enter into a metacognitive process to "examine processes [she] used to think and write in a variety of disciplines and contexts," as defined by the *Framework*. Through her reflection she was responsible to "act on the understanding that learning is shared among the writer and others—students, instructors, and the institution, as well as those engaged in the questions and/or fields in what the writer is interested."

While reflecting on her growth territories, Esme was developing flexible writing processes, also outlined in the *Framework*, to "reflect on how different writing tasks and elements of the writing process contribute to their development as a writer."

instruction appropriately based on individual student needs, thus improving the impact he has on his learners. In addition, that strengthens his relationships with his students as they become more confident with their approaches to writing.

ACTIVITY 6.3:
Final Exam via Reflective Essay

At the end of the trimester, Andy's students have one more opportunity to share their learning. Although so much reflection could be considered a bit overwhelming, this final piece of writing allows students to look, holistically, at their entire portfolio, beginning with their "Literacy Journey" (Activity 2.1) and across multiple assignments. For this final prompt, the instructions are deceptively simple:

- Discuss your growth and effort as a reader, writer, and thinker;
- Share a particular moment of intellectual risk-taking;
- Consider a growth territory that you still need to pursue in the future;
- Share your overall assessment of yourself as a reader, writer, and critical thinker.

One student, Taylor Idema, outlined responses to all these questions in her final essay. In particular, she noted the importance of choice, stating:

First, I feel that through the entirety of the Shakespeare project, I was finally able to grow as a critical thinker and as a writer as a result of my risk-taking. The first risk that I took in that unit, was choosing my topic. Initially, I had no idea what Postmodernism entailed, but it sounded really interesting to me, so I decided to roll with it. I feel that this ended up paying off in the end because my topic became super interesting to me. I was able to truly apply myself to my work in a way that I hadn't before . . .

When I was younger I frequently read throughout my day to

day life, but starting in middle school and throughout high school, I slowly grew away from that habit. This trimester, I was able to find certain books that re-sparked my passion for reading by choosing books that I found to be both interesting and personally relatable. As a result of this, I was able to more than double the number of books I read during the first trimester. In addition, my stamina for reading has also doubled. . . .

. . . When choosing topics to study this trimester, through different projects, I decided to venture into topics that were either extremely intriguing or very personal and vulnerable. This choice definitely paid off in the end and can be cited though many of my final projects. I hope to be able to continue this kind of personal growth into the future- next trimester and beyond!

Taylor's experience is similar to others in that her love for reading and writing at a young age was diminished by a culture of standardized testing, the pressures of grades, and class work that focused more on curriculum than on students. The moments that sparked her growth were when she was offered choice, provided agency, and entrusted with setting her own goals. She read more, wrote more, and began to identify as a writer. In short, she developed a trust that her words had meaning and her voice had value.

For Troy's students, the invitation at the end of the semester was similar, as they wrote a reflective essay. They were asked to "choose two (2) or three (3) items from the 'learning list' that follows and present evidence that demonstrates what you have learned in each of these two or three areas." Adapted from his colleague, Stephanie West-Puckett, this learning list included a number of possibilities that students could explore and, in turn, provide evidence by quoting themselves, snapping screenshots with descriptions, or hyperlinking to the original work.

- A Rhetorical Approach to Composing
  — What do you know now about how to compose a text for a specific audience?
  — What is your evidence that you understand audience, purpose, context, and how to pick the appropriate production strategies for your audience?
  — In what ways is this new knowledge useful to you?

- Academic Skills/Moves
  - What have you learned about creating summaries, annotations, citations, and using evidence to make a point or express an idea?
  - In what ways are these skills useful to you?
- The Research Process
  - Doing your own research
    - What "counts" as research in different disciplines?
    - What method (observation, survey, interview, etc.) have you found most compelling?
    - In what ways would you compare your definition of research after experiencing our course in relation to what you would have described research to be in high school?
  - Finding sources from others
    - What have you learned about finding and evaluating sources?
    - What makes a source credible?
    - How do you go about selecting appropriate sources for your subject matter?
    - In what ways are these skills useful to you?
- Writing Processes (Both In and Out of School)
  - In what instances did you use brainstorming, focusing, and/or drafting effectively? Describe how these practices were helpful to you as you composed your texts.
  - What did you learn about your writing process? In what ways is this information useful to you?
  - How did your metacognitive reflections help you to become a better writer/composer?
- Collaborating with Others
  - What did you learn about how you work in pairs or teams? How can you use what you learned about how you work collaboratively?
  - What did you learn from the peer conferences about getting and giving feedback? In what ways is this information useful to you?
  - How did the peer review process help you as you completed your projects?
- Multimodal Composing
  - What did you learn from composing with some of the following modes of communication: images, videos, graphs, presentations, physical projects?

BOX 6.6: Engagement and Responsibility

A reflective final exam served to engage Taylor in her growth as a writer as she "[found] meanings new to [her] or [built] on existing meanings as a result of new connections," noted in the *Framework*. By examining the work in her portfolio, she fully understood and "recognize[d] [her] own role in learning." The reflective final exam develops critical thinking as students "create multiple kinds of texts to extend and synthesize their thinking," allowing them to demonstrate their learning and celebrate what they've accomplished.

    — How can you apply what you learned in the future?
    — How do these modes differ from each other?
    — Why are these differences important to you?
  • Something Else?
    — What did you learn that is not listed above?

Conclusion

Throughout the course of a class, at the conclusion of a project, and in the fleeting moments of the last few hours together with their students, teachers have a choice to make. They can move from assignment to assignment as students experience a conveyor-belt survey of their education. Or they can choose to linger with their students in a reflective stance to synthesize learning and celebrate growth. We choose to ask our students to stick around a bit longer, bear witness to the growth they have experienced, and celebrate the outcomes of their newfound confidence as they begin to feel more comfortable identifying as writers. Now, that is something worth celebrating!

    As we have in previous chapters, we close this conversation on reflection and celebration with questions for you to consider on your own or in collegial conversation as you, well, reflect on your own use of reflection.

  • How might you, within the structure of your lesson planning, offer students time to reflect on their growth as writers in your classroom? How might you reflect with your students?

- In what ways can you celebrate your students' writing in meaningful and authentic ways?
- How might the words, actions, and experiences you create increase confidence within your writers?
- And, with digital spaces, what might be additional ways we can help move student writing beyond the classroom and into the hands of authentic audiences? How might we encourage others to give positive and substantial feedback to student work?

Professional Learning for the Teacher of Writing

I t is not enough to teach students how to write. Teachers of writing must first be writers who seek out opportunities to connect with other writers. We understand the struggles of a work/life balance and recognize the time commitment to provide students with the type of genuine feedback they need. It takes a lot of energy to be a writing teacher, and where we choose to invest that energy is important. We are convinced that teachers who write make the best writing teachers. As teachers who actively engage in a process of writing, we are equipped to meet both the needs of our students where they are currently and the gentle approach needed to build their confidence.

We, too, need to manage our professional writing motivation, and we are not that different from our students in that regard. Yet we intrinsically know that those teachers who inspired us to write were the ones who themselves wrote. Similarly, those who inspired us to learn were those who actively pursued authentic professional learning opportunities. As Troy, with coauthor Misty Sailors, recently wrote in a literacy leadership brief for the International Literacy Association, "Teachers are not just cogs in the industrial education machine; rather, they are active agents in an immersive, sustained process of learning" (2018, p. 3).

As we have tried to make clear throughout the book, we rely on—and contribute to—two main professional networks: the National Writing Project and the National Council of Teachers of English. Technology also helps in this regard. Shortly after its inception, teacher-writers (many of whom also engage in educational discussions as teacher leaders) realized the power that social media, Twitter in particular, had to connect and amplify voices into teacher-learner communities. Cited by many as the best source for professional development, Twitter is abuzz with chats, opportunities, discussions, and friends who love to learn about writing as much as we do (links are available at the page for this chapter on the authors' website). There are other tools and spaces, too, which we explore below. In sum, engaging in authentic writing opportunities from our professional networks puts us in the *work* of writing, and it reminds us of the positions in which students find themselves in the classroom.

Sustaining your life as a teacher-writer means advocating for your students, for your profession, and for yourself. While we love what large professional networks can do for us, it is much more fulfilling to pull a seat up to the table and enter into the conversations surrounding literacy. Those of us who write for journals, lead presentations, or volunteer time in our networks do it for the same reason you chose to read this book: we are all learning, all the time, together. We feel that being a writer can do the same for other teachers of writing.

Thus, in this final chapter, we explicitly revisit *The Framework for Success in Postsecondary Writing* and *Professional Knowledge for the Teaching of Writing*, describing the ways in which we have pursued our own professional learning, especially as it relates to our work as teacher-writers. As we have throughout the book, we hope that these invitations, this encouragement, will help move you, our colleagues, a little bit out of your comfort zone. As in previous chapters, links mentioned in the text can be found on this chapter's page on the authors' website. Just as we encourage our students to read, write, risk, and share within and beyond our classrooms, we invite you to do so with your learning network. Let's explore the ways in which we position ourselves as writers by setting writing goals, engaging in professional organizations, and embracing a few of the countless activities enabled by the networks of teacher-writers we can find online.

Becoming the Lead Learner/Writer

As we consider the many ways in which we can create confident writers, we need to take the time, space, and energy to create confidence-building opportunities of our own. Certainly, if you are reading this book, you care about your professional growth. Moreover, you view your growth as a catalyst for student growth. As we have reiterated, to be a teacher means you are a student and learner first. As we model what it means to be a good writer, teachers can serve students well by adopting the role of the lead learner.

We have seen the phrase "lead learner" used in a few different places, and we attribute it most to the work of George Couros. A prolific principal, blogger, and speaker, Couros mentioned "Lead Learner" in the title of a January 2011 blog post (Couros, 2011); and we have also seen it more recently in Michael McDowell's work (2018). Even if we can't quite pin down exactly when or where the term first emerged, Andy has taken the idea of being a "lead learner" to heart with his students, using the phrase to describe himself both with them and with colleagues. Though he is appealing broadly to school administrators in his definition, we define what it means to be a "lead learner" in a manner similar to McDowell, who argues that lead learners "model effective learning in their daily practices and short- and long-term decisions" (p. 9). For both Andy and Troy, it is this modeling process—demonstrating for students how they can live rich reading and writing lives—that makes our work particularly rewarding . . . as well as demanding.

A lead learner is someone, like you, who continually pushes their own thinking, engages in friendly dialogues online and in person, takes risks for the benefit of those they encounter, and empowers others to strive to meet their own personal learning goals. Or, as summarized in this concise list from TeachThought's Terry Heick (2018), there are eight attributes that every teacher needs in order to grow:

1. Humility
2. Vision
3. Meaningful collaboration
4. A sense of belonging
5. A sense of priority
6. Diverse ideas and perspectives
7. Pedagogical knowledge
8. Reflection

Our hope is that, in this book, we have shown how these qualities propel us forward in our work. For teacher-writers who act as lead learners, living out the writing processes we tell them to do sends an unmistakable message to students: we practice what we teach. The teachers who have been our greatest inspirations are these kinds of learners. They do not assume to know everything about the teaching of writing; rather, they practice the art by reading more, writing more, risking more, and sharing more. They, like you, are learning.

As lead learners, we must become comfortable with change and living slightly outside of our comfort zone. Living and working in the unknown is not easy for anyone who has become comfortable with their current pedagogy. But, like any endeavor, it begins with surrounding yourself with others who inspire you, withhold judgment, and encourage you to pursue your goals. How we do that, guided by NWP principles, is a process outlined below.

How We Set Goals for Writing

Whenever we set goals for ourselves, it is not in isolation. Typically, we see something that is interesting to us and we strive to emulate mentors. Goal setting is a process that incorporates personal interests with ways of sharing learning along the

TABLE 6.7: Tenets of the NWP Leadership Framework

NWP Leadership Tenets	Ways in Which We Set Goals
Write	• Writing as practice • Writing to learn • Writing to inquire • Writing to reflect
Go public with our practice	• Write articles • Facilitate workshops • Visit other classrooms • Observational rounds • Lesson study • Demo teaching • Publish curriculum • Share on social media
Learn and engage with the profession	• Read research • Contribute by publishing own research • Participate in professional conferences, social media chats, webinars, workshops
Collaborate and respond	• Use learning protocols • Writing groups • Writing retreats
Lead	• Answer calls for proposals • Seek leadership opportunities • Advocate for literacy • Share your work and practices
Advocate	• Writing for or taking action with and on behalf of marginalized students, families, communities, and/or professionals

Source: Adapted by Andrew Schoenborn and Troy Hicks from "NWP Teacher Consultant Badge Framework"

way. It is a social practice used to build personal accountability. As lead learners in the classroom, we use the NWP's "Teacher Consultant Badge Framework" (n.d.b). This framework is a robust tool for goal setting that asks us to read, write, risk, and share—all with the aim of learning and growing.

The tenets of the National Writing Project Leadership Framework remind us that writing with purpose requires agency, choice, reflection, and authenticity. Though not an exhaustive list, we have tried to show how we enact these tenets, by writing for interested and authentic audiences in order to join the conversations happening all around us. Understanding the goals that writers have is important, and knowing that the work happens during the process of writing is important, too. In short, we embrace these tenets, and our lives as teacher-writers, all in an effort toward continuous professional growth.

Become Part of Professional Organizations

While we appreciate the efforts of local school districts and universities to provide professional development for teachers under their leadership, it is nonetheless a challenging task to meet the personal professional needs of its educators. Therefore, we recognize that to receive the energizing nudge we need, we rely on large professional networks to sustain and nurture us. Perhaps it is the NWP's stances, embodied in the idea of "teachers teaching teachers," that we hold so close to our hearts, yet we genuinely believe that teachers' ideas are a benefit to larger literacy communities. We encourage our colleagues to read more, risk more, write more, and share more. It is how we grow as teachers of writing.

It is not the intention of this section to list all the amazing organizations that make it their mission to serve the needs of literacy professionals; we do, however, have a few national and local organizations we claim as our professional homes. Each of them fulfills various professional needs as they sustain our professional lives and maintain the momentum for learning that we desire. Each has robust digital support and opportunities to raise one's voice when entering ongoing conversations about literacy. We view membership in these groups as vital to sustaining and thriving as teacher-writers.

Here we give a bit more background on the National Council of Teachers of English, the International Literacy Association, the National Writing Project, and the International Society for Technology in Education. As with other resources we have shared, links to these professional organizations' home pages can be found on this chapter's page on the authors' website.

Finally, we view these parent organizations as powerful national advocates for literacy and technology, who keep students at the center of their missions. Membership in each is valuable, though somewhat costly. Similarly, their annual conferences are amazing celebrations of teaching, learning, and growing; however, registration and travel fees are expensive, even for those of us who are able to offset some of those expenditures through our employers or grants. Thus, we strongly encourage readers to look at national, regional, state, and local affiliates as a way to enter the professional dialogue, often at a substantially reduced rate.

National Council of Teachers of English (NCTE)

For over one hundred years, NCTE has been devoted to improving the teaching and learning of English and the language arts. "Formed primarily out of protest against overly-specific college entrance requirements and the effects they were having on high school English education," NCTE's roots were formed to "advance access, power, agency, affiliation, and impact for all learners" (National Council of Teachers of English, n.d.). At its core, NCTE is an influential network of educators who dedicate their work to the empowerment of students and teachers. They strive to build on an ever-growing body of knowledge, knowing that literacy is a fundamental change agent. Their peer-reviewed work is steeped in studies, evidence, and practical research. The National Council of Teachers of English creates confident teachers who, in turn, create confident and literate students. In addition to a link to NCTE's main page, we also include a link to a list of state-level affiliates on the authors' website.

International Literacy Association (ILA)

Established in 1956, the International Literacy Association dedicates its work to improving literacy for all through peer-reviewed research, longitudinal studies, and support of educators. It is their mission to "empower educators, inspire students, and encourage leaders with the resources they need to make literacy accessible for all" (International Literacy Association, n.d.). The ILA's long-standing stance of literacy for all encourages educators to write about their practices and work in collaboration to help students live confident literate lives. They know, and we agree, that reading and writing are fundamental rights of every learner. In addition, they recognize the writing connection that will improve access to the world as students learn to enter into larger conversations. Again, a link to the main page and ILA chapters can be found on the authors' website.

National Writing Project (NWP)

Motivated out of the desire to create a different form of professional development for English teachers, and first established in 1974, the National Writing Project's mission "focuses the knowledge, expertise, and leadership of our nation's educators on sustained efforts to improve writing and learning for all learners" (National Writing Project, n.d.a). The NWP honors the brilliant work of teacher-writers with the idea that promising practices should be shared with others so we can all learn. Using the model of "teachers teaching teachers," the NWP actively encourages English teachers to become confident literacy experts who work in collaboration with one another as we read, risk, and share what works to create confident student writers. Participation in an NWP invitational summer institute has often become a career-defining moment for teachers who seek to improve their writing practices and pedagogy. For us, it has fundamentally changed our approach to the teaching of writing. The NWP main page has a link to an interactive map of sites, and the "Complete List of NWP Sites" is linked from this chapter's page on the authors' website, too.

International Society for Technology in Education (ISTE)

What began as a series of "what ifs" about education and technology during a backyard barbeque in 1979 has grown into a network of thought leaders seeking to honor student vision through the intersection of education and technology. The International Society for Technology in Education makes it their mission to "use technology to innovate teaching and learning, accelerate good practice and solve tough problems in education by . . . rethinking education and empowering learners" (International Society for Technology in Education, n.d.). ISTE works in collaboration with teachers who seek to blend promising educational practices with technology for student growth. At its center, members believe that students have a built-in inquiry mindset that can be celebrated as teachers work as guides and collaborators to help students discover interesting ways of writing about and communicating ideas to the world. A list of affiliates and ISTE's home page can be found on the authors' website.

Finally, we encourage teacher-writers to answer the call for both conference proposals and manuscripts, all while leaning on mentors (both texts, as models, and colleagues for feedback and encouragement). Keeping in mind the many conference can be offered as well as calls for proposals in journals and newsletters, we encourage readers to write for one's self, for our students, and for our profession. Teachers' voices are valuable, and we look forward to hearing more voices in the conversation. Though not a comprehensive list, we summarize a number of calls for manuscripts and conference proposals on this chapter's page on the authors' website.

Teacher-Writers Across the Web

We love large professional networks because they refresh our teaching lives, build connections, and generate new ideas. But, after the initial surge, we may settle back into our teaching lives and lose the enthusiasm we had during annual conferences. For us, and for our students, actively seeking authentic writing opportunities is critical to sustaining confident writing lives. Writing for an audience who you know will read what you write changes the writing game.

Perhaps you already have an active writing life, but if you are not sure where to begin, we suggest these entry points to write with and for active audiences. One way is by engaging in writing challenges, another by connecting with and creating your own professional/personal learning network. These networks are crucial for maintaining a sense of momentum and purpose.

Writing, at times, is a lonely endeavor, but when you surround yourself with passionate and practical writing friends you can build a writing momentum on your own terms. The writers we know are kind, compassionate, and understanding. When you know the struggles that come with writing you are better equipped to be a listening ear. Writers also know that writing does not happen without intentional habits and routines that get words moving.

We are convinced that writers help sustain other writers both in the classroom and in professional practice. Connecting again with the *Framework*, we know that developing your own writing routine and habit demonstrates to your students that actively participating with writing groups creates a sense of responsibility to "recognize [your] own role in learning" and "act on the understanding that learning is shared among the writer and others—students, instructors, and the institution, as well as those engaged in the questions and/or fields in which the writer is interested" (p. 5).

Moreover, we have come to learn that writing, conferring, and sharing with other teacher-writers is a metacognitive endeavor. We "examine processes [we] use to think and write in a variety of disciplines and contexts; reflect on the texts that [we] have produced in a variety of contexts; connect choices [we] have made in texts to audiences and purposes for which texts are intended; and use what [we] learn from reflections on one writing project to improve writing on subsequent projects" (p. 5).

Here are some approaches that we have found to be valuable in our own growth as teacher-writers; even more specific strategies can be found in the book Troy wrote with his own writing group, *Coaching Teacher-Writers* (Hicks et al., 2016).

Writing Challenges

Teacher-writers know the difficulty of starting and maintaining a writing habit—after all, we each live busy lives that pull us away from our writing. Yet there are plenty of opportunities asking us to be pulled into writing. Thousands of teacher-writers participate in writing challenges that take advantage of teaching schedules. During these challenges we write, share, support, comment on, and celebrate a teacher-writer life. While this section does not list every opportunity to build a teacher-writer community, it offers opportunities we, and others, have found that rekindle our joy for writing. Collaboration through these challenges can be a beautiful alignment of purpose and intent that will move you and your students to places that seem out of reach, when, in reality, they are only a few keystrokes and digital connections away.

For a more complete description of each activity and the challenges themselves, the links are available on this chapter's page on the authors' website.

Stacey Shubitz and Ruth Ayres's Slice of Life Story Challenge

Stacey Shubitz co-founded the Two Writing Teachers blog in 2007 with the belief that "teachers who teach writing should write, not out of obligation or duty, but rather out of the knowledge that strong teachers of writing are effective when they live the life they expect of their students" (Two Writer Teachers, n.d.). The "Slice of Life Story Challenge" offers teachers an opportunity to begin and build their writing habit. Teacher-writers can join this vibrant community of writers who engage in low-risk, high-reward opportunities.

Kate Messner's Teachers Write Challenge

As teachers of writers, we agree with Kate Messner, known for her award-winning picture books and YA novels, who believes that "people who teach writing are most effective when they are truly writers themselves" (Messner, 2018). She also knows that writers need opportunities to be surrounded by other authors, teachers, and librarians to support, share practices, and encourage others to lift their voices. As a former middle-school teacher who spent fifteen years writing beside teachers, Messner understands that the summer slide can affect teachers as well as students. Which is why each summer she launches a free online teacher writer camp. Join in each July and August!

National Novel Writing Month

Founded by Chris Baty in 1999, and with its roots in the San Francisco Bay area, the month of November brings with it National Novel Writing Month (NaNoWriMo). This challenge encourages writers from across the country to rise up, kickstart their writing habit, put their collective butts in the seat, and get to work writing. NaNoWriMo believes in "the transformational power of creativity. We provide the structure, community, and encouragement to help people find their voices, achieve creative goals, and build new worlds—on and off the page" (National Novel Writing Month, n.d.).

As a quick personal example, Andy has participated in NaNoWriMo but always had difficulties finding writing buddies, and so he moved his work online (as will be described in more detail later in the chapter). His group, comprising teacher-writers from Maine, Wisconsin, New York, Virginia, and Michigan, all agreed on how challenging it is to find writer-types who actually want to write, yet the opportunities for online camaraderie, encouragement, and feedback made NaNoWriMo possible.

Teach Write Academy

Jennifer Laffin, a former classroom teacher, recognized that it wasn't until she became a teacher-writer herself that she truly understood how to teach writing. In 2017 she founded Teach Write LLC "to help give teachers the confidence and support they need to develop their own writing habit so that they can become stronger teachers of writers" (Teach Write LLC, n.d.). Teacher-writers from across the country join Zoom writing sessions to talk about their writing goals, accomplishments, and celebrations as teachers of writers.

In addition to creating online spaces for teacher-writers to meet, write, and grow together, Laffin's #TeachWrite Chat Blog invites guest bloggers to weigh in on monthly themes such as "We Are Writers," "Sharing Our Writing Lives," and

"Maintaining Our Writing Momentum." These are the guest blog posts where Andy cut his teacher-writing teeth, and links to find out more are on this chapter's page of the authors' website.

Guest Blogging

Though not a "challenge" in the sense of having a specific timeline and accountability structure in place like those listed above, there are also numerous opportunities to blog. As we've said, writers need an audience. Short of beginning one's own blog, there are plenty of platforms to write for an established audience as a guest blogger. What follows are a few of our favorite places to learn from other teacher-writers, give back to the profession, and write for an audience tailored to your love of education.

We have collaborated on presentations with peers met via Twitter as we used digital tools to plan, promote, and provide spaces to share our learning and meet in real life. Again, links are provided on the authors' website for each of these.

Build Your Stack Blog (NCTE)

#BuildYourStack is a teacher-writer opportunity offered by the National Council of Teachers of English and curated by its members (Various Build Your Stack Authors, n.d.).

Recognizing the potent power of book choice and book pairings, the aim is to help "teachers build their book knowledge and their classroom libraries" with current texts sure to resonate with students of all ages. There are multiple ways you can write for #BuildYourStack that vary in word count:

- Build Your Stack resource posts include instructional resources and recommended books (400–600 words);
- Build Your Stack book highlights include recommended books (150 words) to be used as NCTE Facebook posts or features in NCTE INBOX;
- Build Your Stack videos accompany book recommendations (2–3 minutes for resource posts and one-minute book highlights).

Although current guest blog post submissions are limited to NCTE members, this is a low-pressure, high-impact way to get started as a teacher-writer.

Moving Writers Blog

Founded by teacher-writers Rebekah O'Dell and Allison Marchetti (first mentioned in Chapter 3), with the belief "that teaching is about much, much more than transmitting skills and knowledge. We believe in teaching that changes students at their core," *Moving Writers* is a blog dedicated to the power of mentor texts as a transformative guide for all writers (O'Dell & Marchetti, 2016). Built on the understanding that students are surrounded by texts that pull readers in and that mentor texts teach both students and teachers how to grow their writing craft, *Moving Writers* invites teacher-writers to share their mentor text success stories as guest bloggers.

Nerdy Book Club Blog

Shared first in Chapter 3 as a resource for authentic student writing and publishing, the Nerdy Book Club needs teacher-writers, too. Longtime advocates of choice reading and student access to books, Donalyn Miller, Colby Sharp, Katherine Sokolowski, and Cindy Minnich recognize that there are many wonderful books in the world readers may miss the chance to read. As teacher-writers themselves, they encourage readers to share their love of reading by inviting guest bloggers to write for them. They outline various topics such as "Reading Lives," "New Book Reviews," "Retro Reviews," "Pay It Forward posts," and "Top Ten posts," and they include an interactive Google Form for submitting ideas (Nerdy Book Club, 2014).

Writers Who Care

Founded with the intent "that writing instruction is essential for students across grade levels and content areas and that writing is a way to help students change their worlds," the *Writers Who Care* blog provides their readers—and writers—with the opportunity to "learn about writing, the teaching of writing, and the power of engaging young writers in craft and story" (Members of the Commission on Writing Teacher Education, 2013). The blog editorial team employs a peer-review process and coaches writers through each stage of the process, from initial ideas to final posts.

Connecting with PLNs

Finally, we offer some insight on three different social media tools that we use to connect with colleagues: Facebook, Twitter, and video conferencing. As with all the opportunities outlined in this chapter, choosing the particular tools, times, and activities in which to engage is a continual balancing act. After reading the previous sections, it can already feel overwhelming to consider the many possibilities for writing. Yet we want to reiterate the point here that having a network (whether a single writing partner or an entire group of like-minded colleagues) is critical for pushing one's thinking and making our practice public.

Facebook Groups

Nearly ubiquitous in nature and ever ready at our fingertips (perhaps too much, as recent trends in "detoxing" our digital lives make clear), Facebook is, still, a powerful platform for creating a personal learning network. Social networks become what you choose to make of them; for Andy, Facebook had long been just a digital scrapbook where he shared pictures and videos of family events. Today, his "extended family" is sprawling and Facebook had become the de facto place to keep in contact with colleagues from around the world.

Andy admits it felt risky at first, but he began sending friend requests to writing mentors, and, to his surprise, some of them accepted his requests. His feed began to fill up with mentors and he began to see different sides of who these people are, including the way they process information. By surrounding himself with educators he admired, he began to notice positive ways in which his thinking shifted, many of which began to make their way into his classroom.

There are countless numbers of Facebook groups in which educators add to the conversation, ask questions, participate, gather information, or jump at opportunities for publication as they become available. It can be a challenge to fully participate in all the groups because there is a lot of activity. Nonetheless, the generosity of those in the groups is worth seeking membership. Other platforms, like Participate, offer similar social spaces, and we have links to a few of our favorite spaces on this chapter's page on the authors' website.

More recently, with the advent of tools like Voxer, which is specifically focused on sharing voice-based messages, and group chats that can happen in iMessage or WhatsApp, educators have even more options. For instance, in a blog post aptly titled "How Voxer changed my personal AND professional life," National Board Certified teacher Angela Watson notes that Voxer allows you to leave messages on the go, that you can really hear tone of voice, and that you only talk with people with whom you have chosen to establish a connection (Watson, 2014).

We encourage you to seek groups that feel inclusive of your needs and personal goals. In these groups, teachers share stories, resources, and insights in productive ways. These groups are meant to connect, collaborate, and share. Community members genuinely want to see you succeed and rely on one another to reach the collective goals of everyone involved: student achievement.

Regardless of the means for communication, groups that connect via Facebook, Voxer, Participate, or other platforms provide us, as educators, with a great deal of support and enlightenment. We appreciate the relationships that have formed through these groups, especially those that continue to move us forward as teacher-writers.

Twitter Chats

Twitter invokes many preconceived notions, mainly because we hear the stories of celebrities, politicians, and reporters who have used it. Indeed, it can be a place for shameless plugs and an arena for uncivilized arguments. However, many educators use Twitter as a space for professional learning, and some who are very active can ask a question of their followers and, within seconds, be bombarded with a flurry of responses.

More useful, we feel, are Twitter chats. It is difficult for both of us to remember the very first Twitter chat in which we participated, though it likely came through invitation. During that first conversation, as it happened for Andy, he recalls simply watching as many brilliant educators shared their ideas. They posed thought-provoking questions while others responded with insight and resources. They retweeted or liked ideas that resonated. Beyond the screen, it is likely that they were smiling, maybe even laughing from time to time. Meanwhile, he lurked, and learned.

The next time Andy decided to join a chat, it began as usual by asking participants to share their name, what they teach, and where they are from. Perhaps it was to ease his worry, but at the end of his introductory chat tweet he added, "I am learning." To his surprise, a few people replied with affirmation and encouragement. The chat took off in a flurry of tweets and it was hard to keep up. But he chose to follow along at his own pace, realizing he did not have to read every single tweet to have an understanding of the conversation.

Many educators who take to Twitter have similar stories, and there are, of course, some who have sworn off it over the years. Yet, as a go-to source for inspiration and connection, Twitter—and, more specifically, the dozens of specific Twitter chats that educators organize and participate in—are useful in their own way. In contrast to the Facebook groups, Twitter always feels more ephemeral, and it may not be the most useful space, depending on your preferences. Still, these are worth exploring; and, like the Facebook groups mentioned above, the links are available at this chapter's page on the authors' website.

Writing Groups via Video Conference

For many years, both Andy and Troy have participated in various forms of writing groups that connect via video conference. Skype, Google Hangouts, Facetime, WebEx, and many other video-conferencing solutions can work; we prefer Zoom for its ease of use, connectivity options, and minimalist design. This makes the connections with friends more personal, and committing to regular times and days for discussing our writing, or simply being in the same virtual space while writing, can be powerful.

Admittedly, video conferencing is intimidating at first, because you cannot prep yourself too much for the interactions. As such, the candid nature and the vulnerability these conversations produce is just what a writer needs to gain comfort learning, writing, and sharing with fellow writers, all of whom are battling their own writing struggles. After a while, the comfort levels increase, bonds are formed, and writing gets done. In that sense, few things match the intimate power of video-conference writing groups.

Over the years, we have experienced small writing groups of two to three people, medium-sized writing groups of four to six people, large writing groups of seven to ten people, and massive writing groups of twenty-plus people. All serve their own purpose, but we find the small- to medium-sized groups to be just about right. In these settings, you are able to interact with everyone in the group, get to know a bit about them, and share your thoughts without inadvertently speaking over someone.

Andy uses his writing group time as, well, time to write. In an hour-long format, he and his colleagues usually spend about ten minutes introducing themselves and catching up on news, then each will share what he or she plans to work on during the time together. This is followed by a blissful thirty to forty minutes of writing with microphones on mute. Near the end of the hour, all participants hop back on and discuss how they have met individual goals for the time together. Critical to Andy's writing group experience is creating a judgment-free zone. They come together for one reason only—to write—and it is wonderful.

Troy typically structures his writing group time in a slightly different format. Prior to the group meeting, the author on whose work they will be providing feedback shares a document, usually a Google Doc, with the group. Ideally, this happens at least a day ahead of time, but sometimes even with a few hours' notice, group members will have time to read, offer marginal comments, and have a sense of what the writer is working on. Then, during the meeting itself, the author opens up opportunities for conversation by posing specific questions about his or her writing, seeking input from group members. Members are able to take notes and collaborate on the document, giving the writer feedback and revision suggestions.

Being and Becoming Teacher-Writers

Hearkening back to our introduction, we again invite our readers to consider what it means to be and become a teacher-writer. Although it can be argued that this kind of connectivity creates a work-life imbalance, none of these interactions with our personal learning networks are required. Our writing and collaborative spaces vary widely and happen in many different places. The benefit of learning in openly networked spaces is the freedom it creates to learn when you want, at the pace you desire, and with people who inspire you whenever and wherever you participate.

Still, if someone is wondering about how and why participating in these learning networks and becoming a teacher-writer is important, here we make a final, direct appeal:

> At first glance you may feel overwhelmed by all the writing opportunities available. You may think all of this is way outside your comfort zone and, depending on how you view yourself as a writer, it may very well be.
>
> But the truth is, at some point for every writer, they felt the same way. That voice you hear, the one that tells you "You are not ready for this" or "You can't do this . . ."—you know that is the voice of your inner critic, the judge.
>
> The transition from thinking about the idea of writing to owning the identity of being a writer is smoothed when you surround yourself with other writers. We know all too well the voice of the judge, and we also know that encouragement, celebration, and having others cheering you on will turn down the volume of the judge.
>
> Fortunately, there are plenty of opportunities to grow your professional learning network as well as build your own confidence as a teacher-writer. Please join us in being and becoming a teacher-writer.
>
> We look forward to hearing your voice in the unending conversation.
>
> *Andy and Troy*

References

Achebe, C. (1958). *Things Fall Apart*. Oxford, UK: Heinemann.

Allyn, P. (2015, July 16). Reading Is Like Breathing In; Writing Is Like Breathing Out. Retrieved May 13, 2019, from Literacy Daily website: https://literacyworldwide.org/blog/literacy-daily/2015/07/16/reading-is-like-breathing-in-writing-is-like-breathing-out.

Anderson, J. (2011). *Ten Things Every Writer Needs to Know*. Portland, ME: Stenhouse Publishers.

Anderson, J., & Dean, D. (2014). *Revision Decisions: Talking Through Sentences and Beyond*. Portland, ME: Stenhouse Publishers.

Applebee, A. N. (1981). *Writing in the Secondary School: English and the Content Areas./* Urbana, IL: National Council of Teachers of English.

Applebee, A. N., & Langer, J. A. (2011). A snapshot of writing instruction in middle schools and high schools. *English Journal, 100*(6), 14.

Atwell, N. (1998a). *In the Middle: New Understandings About Writing, Reading, and Learning, Second Edition*. Portsmouth, NH: Heinemann.

Atwell, N. (2014). *In the Middle: A Lifetime of Learning About Writing, Reading, and Adolescents, Third Edition*. Portsmouth, NH: Heinemann.

Bailey, E. (2018, September 7). My E.L.A. Journey; From Beginning to Other Beginnings. Retrieved April 20, 2019, from https://eb11000.edublogs.org/2018/09/07/my-e-l-a-journey-from-beginning-to-other-beginnings/.

Beers, K., & Probst, R. E. (2017). *Disrupting Thinking: Why How We Read Matters*. New York: Scholastic Incorporated.

Blair, D. (2015, February 5). *Finland to teach typing rather than handwriting in schools*. Retrieved from http://www.telegraph.co.uk/news/worldnews/europe/finland/11391999/Finland-to-teach-typing-rather-than-handwriting-in-schools.html.

Bomer, K. (2016). *The Journey Is Everything: Teaching Essays That Students Want to Write for People Who Want to Read Them*. Portsmouth, NH: Heinemann.

Boud, D., Keogh, R., & Walker, D. (1985). Promoting Reflection in Learning: A Model. In D. Boud, Keogh, R., & Walker, D. (Eds.), *Reflection: Turning Experience Into Learning*. London: Routledge, pp. 18–40.

Branch, J. (2012). Snow Fall: The Avalanche at Tunnel Creek. Retrieved February 11, 2014, from http://www.nytimes.com/projects/2012/snow-fall/.

Brundin, J. (2014, July 29). Q & A: Is it bad if children don't learn handwriting? Retrieved July 13, 2016, from Colorado Public Radio website: http://www.cpr.org/news/story/q -it-bad-if-children-dont-learn-handwriting.

Burke, J. (2003). *Writing Reminders: Tools, Tips, and Techniques*. Portsmouth, NH: Heinemann.

Burke, J. (2012). *The English Teacher's Companion, Fourth Edition: A Completely New Guide to Classroom, Curriculum, and the Profession, Fourth Edition*. Portsmouth, NH: Heinemann.

Burke, K. (1974). *The Philosophy of Literary Form, Third Edition*. Berkeley: University of California Press.

Cavanagh, S. R. (2016). *The Spark of Learning: Energizing the College Classroom with the Science of Emotion*. Morgantown, WV: West Virginia University Press.

Chemin, A. (2014, December 16). Handwriting vs typing: is the pen still mightier than the keyboard? *The Guardian*. Retrieved from https://www.theguardian.com/ science/2014/dec/16/cognitive-benefits-handwriting-decline-typing.

Coelho, P. (1988). *The Alchemist, 30th Anniversary Edition*. New York: HarperCollins.

Common Core State Standards Initiative. (n.d.). English Language Arts Standards » Introduction » Students Who are College and Career Ready in Reading, Writing, Speaking, Listening, & Language. Retrieved November 24, 2018, from Common Core State Standards Initiative website: http://www.corestandards.org/ELA-Literacy/introduction/ students-who-are-college-and-career-ready-in-reading-writing-speaking-listening -language/.

Council of Writing Program Administrators, National Council of Teachers of English, & National Writing Project. (2011, January). Framework for Success in Postsecondary Writing. Retrieved August 12, 2012, from http://wpacouncil.org/framework/.

Couros, G. (2011, January 9). Evolution of a Lead learner. Retrieved December 15, 2018, from The Principal of Change website: https://georgecouros.ca/blog/archives/1646.

Cupryk, R. (n.d.). *Literary Theories: A Sampling of Critical Lenses*. Retrieved from http://www .mpsaz.org/rmhs/staff/rkcupryk/aa_jr/files/microsoft_word_-_literary_theories.pdf.

Dai, H., Milkman, K. L., & Riis, J. (2014). The Fresh Start Effect: Temporal Landmarks Motivate Aspirational Behavior. *Management Science*, *60*(10), 2563–2582. https://doi .org/10.1287/mnsc.2014.1901

Davis, T. (2018, November 16). Marking Period 2 Reading Analysis. Retrieved May 22, 2019, from AP LIT Blogfolio website: https://tori4476.edublogs.org/2018/11/16/ marking-period-2-reading-analysis/

Dawson, C. M. (2016). *The Teacher-Writer: Creating Writing Groups for Personal and Professional Growth*. New York, NY: Teachers College Press.

Duenes, S., Kissane, E., Kueneman, A., Myint, J., Roberts, G., & Spangler, C. (n.d.). How We Made Snow Fall: A Q&A with the New York Times team. Retrieved May 21, 2019, from Source OpenNews Project website: https://source.opennews.org/articles/how-we-made-snow-fall/

Dweck, C. S. (2007). *Mindset: The New Psychology of Success* (Reprint, Updated edition). New York: Ballantine Books.

EveryDayMusicTV. (2013). *DAY298 - Shane Koyczan and Hannah Epperson - Remember How We Forgot.* Retrieved from https://www.youtube.com/watch?v=NBVJuA0jr6Y

Falk, D. (1995). Preflection: A Strategy for Enhancing Reflection. *NSEE Quarterly*, 13.

Finkelstein, E. (2013, August 2). PechaKucha 20x20 - How To Create Slides. Retrieved May 20, 2019, from PechaKucha 20x20 website: https://www.pechakucha.com/presentations/how-to-create-slides

Flannery, M. E. (2014, March 10). The Kids Are All Right: Meet the Next Generation of Social Justice Activists. Retrieved May 16, 2019, from NEA Today website: http://neatoday.org/2014/03/10/the-kids-are-all-right-meet-the-next-generation-of-social-justice-activists/

Flaubert, G. (1856). *Madame Bovary*. Bantam Books.

Fletcher, R. (2013). *What a Writer Needs, Second Edition* (2 edition). Portsmouth, NH: Boynton/Cook.

Fletcher, R. (2017). *Joy Write: Cultivating High-impact, Low-stakes Writing*. Heinemann.

Fried, R. L. (2005). *The Game of School: Why We All Play It, How It Hurts Kids, and What It Will Take to Change It*. San Francisco, CA: Jossey-Bass.

Gallagher, K. (2006). *Teaching Adolescent Writers*. Portland, Me: Stenhouse Publishers.

Gallagher, K. (2011). *Write like this: Teaching real-world writing through modeling and mentor texts*. Portland, ME: Stenhouse Publishers.

Gallagher, K., & Kittle, P. (2018). *180 Days: Two Teachers and the Quest to Engage and Empower Adolescents*. Heinemann.

Geisthardt, H. (2018, April 14). Top Ten LGBTQ+ YA Novels for All Tastes. Retrieved June 10, 2019, from Nerdy Book Club website: https://nerdybookclub.wordpress.com/2018/04/14/top-ten-lgbtq-ya-novels-for-all-tastes-by-haylee-geisthardt/

Goldberg, N. (2010). *Writing Down the Bones: Freeing the Writer Within* (1st (Expanded)). Shambhala.

Goodman, S., & Fine, M. (2018). *It's Not About Grit: Trauma, Inequity, and the Power of Transformative Teaching*. New York: Teachers College Press.

Graff, G., & Birkenstein, C. (2018). *They Say / I Say: The Moves That Matter in Academic Writing, Fourth Edition*. New York: Norton.

Graham, S., Fitzgerald, J., Friedrich, L., Greene, K., Kim, J. S., & Booth Olson, C. (2016, November). *Teaching secondary students to write effectively (NCEE 2017-4002)*. Retrieved from https://ies.ed.gov/ncee/wwc/PracticeGuide/22

Graham, S., & Perin, D. (2007). *Writing next: Effective strategies to improve writing of adolescents in middle and high schools* (p. 77). Retrieved from Carnegie Corporation of NewYork website: http://www.all4ed.org/files/WritingNext.pdf

Gunelius, S. (2019, May 20). Do You Know What a Vlog Is? Retrieved May 27, 2019, from Lifewire website: https://www.lifewire.com/what-is-a-vlog-3476285

Hattie, J. (2011). *Visible Learning for Teachers: Maximizing Impact on Learning* (1 edition). London ; New York: Routledge.

Heard, G. (2014). *The Revision Toolbox, Second Edition: Teaching Techniques That Work* (2 edition). Portsmouth, NH: Heinemann.

Heick, T. (2018, October 17). 8 Things Every Teacher Needs In Order To Grow. Retrieved December 15, 2018, from TeachThought website: https://www.teachthought.com/pedagogy/8-lessons-teacher-growth/

Hesse, H. (1922). *Siddhartha*. Bantam Books.

Hiaasen, M. (n.d.). *Literary Criticism: Questions for a Variety of Approaches.* Retrieved from https://herefordhs.bcps.org/UserFiles/Servers/Server_3705599/File/Academics/English/Literary_Criticism_Generic_questions.pdf

Hicks, T. (2013). *Crafting digital writing: Composing texts across media and genres.* Portsmouth, NH: Heinemann.

Hicks, T., Busch-Grabmeyer, E., Hyler, J., & Smoker, A. (2013). Write, respond, repeat: A model for teachers' professional writing groups in a digital age. In K. Pytash, R. E. Ferdig, & T. Rasinski (Eds.), *Preparing teachers to teach writing using technology* (pp. 149–161). Retrieved from http://press.etc.cmu.edu/files/Teachers-Writing-Technology-Pytash_Ferdig_Rasinski_etal-web.pdf

Hicks, T., & Sailors, M. (2018). *Democratizing professional growth with teachers: From development to learning* (No. 9437). Retrieved from International Literacy Association website: https://literacyworldwide.org/docs/default-source/where-we-stand/ila-democratizing-professional-growth-with-teachers.pdf

Hicks, T., Whitney, A. E., Fredricksen, J., & Zuidema, L. (2016). *Coaching Teacher-Writers: Practical Steps to Nurture Professional Writing.* New York, NY: Teachers College Press.

Hillocks, G. (1986). *Research on Written Composition: New Directions for Teaching.* National Conference on Research in English.

Hobbs, R. (2017). *Create to Learn: Introduction to Digital Literacy.* Hoboken, NJ, USA: Wiley-Blackwell.

Hopkins, E. M. (1912). Can Good Composition Teaching Be Done under Present Conditions? *English Journal*, *1*(1), 1–8. https://doi.org/10.2307/800827

Hurston, Z. N. (1937). *Their Eyes Were Watching God.* Harper Collins.

Interagency Working Group on Youth Programs. (n.d.). Youth Topics: Mental Health Prevalence. Retrieved May 16, 2019, from Youth.gov website: https://youth.gov/youth-topics/youth-mental-health/prevalance-mental-health-disorders-among-youth

International Literacy Association. (n.d.). About Us & Mission. Retrieved May 25, 2019, from https://www.literacyworldwide.org/about-us

International Society for Technology in Education. (n.d.). Be Bold with Us. Retrieved May 25, 2019, from https://www.iste.org/about/about-iste

Jago, C. (2018). *The Book in Question: Why and How Reading Is in Crisis*. Portsmouth, NH: Heinemann.

Jiang, J. (2018, August 22). How Teens and Parents Navigate Screen Time and Device Distractions. Retrieved September 14, 2018, from Pew Research Center: Internet, Science & Tech website: http://www.pewinternet.org/2018/08/22/how-teens-and-parents-navigate-screen-time-and-device-distractions/

Johnston, P. H. (2004). *Choice Words: How Our Language Affects Children's Learning*. Stenhouse Publishers.

Julia Amting. (2018). *Digital Identity Narrative - Julia Amting*. Retrieved from https://www.youtube.com/watch?v=uJnshv2nPJ0&feature=youtu.be

King, S. (2010). *On Writing: 10th Anniversary Edition: A Memoir of the Craft* (Anniversary edition). New York: Scribner.

Kittle, P. (2008). *Write beside them: Risk, voice, and clarity in high school writing*. Portsmouth, NH: Heinemann.

Kittle, P. (2013). *Book love: developing depth, stamina, and passion in adolescent readers*. Portsmouth, NH: Heinemann.

Klein Dytham Architecture. (n.d.). Frequently Asked Questions | Pecha Kucha. Retrieved June 15, 2019, from PechaKucha 20x20 website: https://www.pechakucha.com/faq

Koyczan, S. (n.d.). *Remember How We Forgot*. Retrieved from https://genius.com/Shane-koyczan-remember-how-we-forgot-lyrics

Lambert, J. (2010). *Digital Storytelling Cookbook*. Retrieved from https://wrd.as.uky.edu/sites/default/files/cookbook.pdf

Lamott, A. (1995). *Bird by Bird: Some Instructions on Writing and Life* (1 edition). New York: Anchor.

Marchetti, A., & O'Dell, R. (2015). *Writing with Mentors: How to Reach Every Writer in the Room Using Current, Engaging Mentor Texts*. Portsmouth, NH: Heinemann.

Martin, T. M. (2016, August 23). #BookSnaps – Snapping for Learning. Retrieved May 13, 2019, from Tara M Martin website: https://www.tarammartin.com/booksnaps-snapping-for-learning/

McDonald, J. P., Mohr, N., Dichter, A., & McDonald, E. C. (2013). *The Power of Protocols: An Educator's Guide to Better Practice, Third Edition* (Third edition). New York: Teachers College Press.

McDowell, M. (2018). *The Lead Learner: Improving Clarity, Coherence, and Capacity for All* (First edition). Thousand Oaks, California: Corwin.

McGee, P. (2017). *Feedback That Moves Writers Forward: How to Escape Correcting Mode to Transform Student Writing* (1 edition). Thousand Oaks, California: Corwin.

Members of the Commission on Writing Teacher Education. (2013, August 5). About | Writers Who Care Blog. Retrieved May 27, 2019, from Teachers, Profs, Parents: Writers Who Care website: https://writerswhocare.wordpress.com/about/

Merriam-Webster Online Dictionary. (n.d.). Definition of Invitation. Retrieved April 4, 2019, from https://www.merriam-webster.com/dictionary/invitation

Messner, K. (2018). Teachers Write 2018! Retrieved May 27, 2019, from https://www
.katemessner.com/teachers-write/

Miller, D., & Sharp, C. (2018). *Game Changer! Book Access for All Kids.* Scholastic
Professional.

Murray, D. (1981). Making Meaning Clear: The Logic of Revision. *Journal of Basic Writing, 3*(3), 33–40.

National Commission on Writing for America's Families, Schools, and Colleges. (2003).
The Neglected "R": The Need for a Writing Revolution. Retrieved December 21, 2008,
from http://www.writingcommission.org/prod_downloads/writingcom/neglectedr.pdf

National Council of Teachers of English. (n.d.). About Us. Retrieved May 25, 2019, from
NCTE website: http://www2.ncte.org/about/

National Council of Teachers of English. (2016a). *Professional Knowledge for the Teaching
of Writing.* Retrieved from National Council of Teachers of English website: http://
www2.ncte.org/statement/teaching-writing/

National Council of Teachers of English. (2016b, February 28). Professional Knowledge
for the Teaching of Writing. Retrieved July 1, 2018, from NCTE website: http://
www2.ncte.org/statement/teaching-writing/

National Novel Writing Month. (n.d.). National Novel Writing Month. Retrieved May
27, 2019, from http://nanowrimo.org/about

National School Reform Faculty. (2017). Critical Friends Groups: Purpose and Work. Retrieved
May 21, 2019, from https://www.nsrfharmony.org/wp-content/uploads/2017/10/cfg_
purpose_work_0.pdf

National School Reform Faculty. (2019). What are protocols? Why use them? Retrieved
December 14, 2017, from https://nsrfharmony.org/whatareprotocols/

National Writing Project. (n.d.a). About NWP. Retrieved May 25, 2019, from https://
www.nwp.org/cs/public/print/doc/about.csp

National Writing Project. (n.d.b). *NWP Teacher Consultant Badge Framework: A Product
Of The Building New Pathways To Leadership Initiative.* Retrieved from https://s16491
.pcdn.co/wp-content/uploads/2018/08/NWP-Social-Practices-Framework.pdf

Nelson, J. (2015). *I'll Give You the Sun* (Reprint edition). New York, New York: Speak.

Nerdy Book Club. (2014, February 27). Want to Be A Nerdy Blogger? Retrieved May 27,
2019, from Nerdy Book Club website: https://nerdybookclub.wordpress.com/want-to
-be-a-nerdy-blogger/

Newkirk, T. (2017). *Embarrassment: And the Emotional Underlife of Learning.* Portsmouth,
NH: Heinemann.

O'Dell, R., & Marchetti, A. (2016, April 7). Our Beliefs & Our Mission. Retrieved May
27, 2019, from Moving Writers website: https://movingwriters.org/about/our-beliefs
-our-mission/

Olio, D., & The Teaching Channel. (2014). *Critical Friends: Collaborating as Writers.* Retrieved
from https://www.teachingchannel.org/video/student-writing-peer-review-nea

O'Neill, L. (2016). *Asking for It.* Quercus Editions Limited.

Paris, D., & Alim, H. S. (Eds.). (2017). *Culturally Sustaining Pedagogies: Teaching and Learning for Justice in a Changing World*. New York: Teachers College Press.

Pink, D. H. (2018). *When: The Scientific Secrets of Perfect Timing*. New York: Riverhead Books.

Reed, D., & Hicks, T. (2015). *Research Writing Rewired: Lessons That Ground Students' Digital Learning*. Thousand Oaks: Corwin.

Robinson, S. K. (2013, April). Transcript of "How to escape education's death valley." Retrieved April 20, 2019, from TED.com website: https://www.ted.com/talks/ ken_robinson_how_to_escape_education_s_death_valley/transcript

Romano, T. (2000). *Blending Genre, Altering Style: Writing Multigenre Papers*. Portsmouth, NH: Boynton/Cook.

Sackstein, S. (2017). *Peer Feedback in the Classroom: Empowering Students to Be the Experts*. Alexandria, Virginia, USA: ASCD.

Schoenborn, A. (2014). Authentic Writing Through Digital Feedback. In R. E. Ferdig, T. V. Rasinski, & K. E. Pytash (Eds.), *Using Technology to Enhance Writing: Innovative Approaches to Literacy Instruction* (pp. 221–226). Bloomington, IN: Solution Tree.

Schoenborn, A. (2018). The Value of Authentic Feedback. In K. Lindblom & L. Christenbury (Eds.), *Continuing the Journey 2: Becoming a Better Teacher of Authentic Writing* (pp. 120–122). Urbana, IL: National Council of Teachers of English.

Shannon, P. (2013). *Closer Readings of the Common Core: Asking Big Questions About the English/Language Arts Standards* (1 edition). Portsmouth, NH: Heinemann.

Sheils, M. (1975). Why Johnny can't write. *Newsweek*, *92*(8), 58–65.

Shubitz, S. (n.d.). Mission | Two Writing Teachers. Retrieved January 9, 2020, from TWO WRITING TEACHERS website: https://twowritingteachers.org/our-mission/

Sinek, S. (2009). *Start with why: How Great Leaders Inspire Everyone to Take Action*. Penguin.

Tchudi, S., & NCTE Committee on Alternatives to Grading Student Writing. (1997). *Alternatives to grading student writing*. Urbana, Ill: National Council of Teachers of English.

Teach Write LLC. (n.d.). About Teach Write. Retrieved May 27, 2019, from Teachers as Writers | Teach Write LLC website: https://www.teachwrite.org/about-us

Thomas, A. (2017). *The Hate U Give* (First Edition Later Printing edition). New York, NY: Balzer + Bray.

Turner, K. H., & Hicks, T. (2015). *Connected Reading: Teaching Adolescent Readers in a Digital World*. Urbana, IL: National Council of Teachers of English.

United States Department of Education. (2002). Introduction: No child left behind. Retrieved from http://www.nclb.gov/next/overview/index.html

VanDerwater, A. L. (2017). *Poems Are Teachers: How Studying Poetry Strengthens Writing in All Genres*. Portsmouth, NH: Heinemann.

Various Build Your Stack Authors. (n.d.). Build Your Stack Archives. Retrieved May 27, 2019, from National Council of Teachers of English website: http://www2.ncte.org/ blog/tag/build-your-stack/

Vega, V., & Robb, M. (2019). *The Common Sense Census: Inside the 21st-Century Classroom*. Retrieved from Common Sense Media website: https://www.commonsensemedia .org/sites/default/files/uploads/research/2019-educator-census-inside-the-21st-century -classroom_1.pdf

Warner, J. (2018). *Why They Can't Write: Killing the Five-Paragraph Essay and Other Necessities*. Johns Hopkins University Press.

Watson, A. (2014, August 16). How Voxer changed my personal AND professional life. Retrieved January 5, 2019, from The Cornerstone For Teachers website: https:// thecornerstoneforteachers.com/bright-ideas-voxer/

West-Puckett, S. (n.d.). MakerComp: Writing, Making, Composing the World. Retrieved September 15, 2018, from Writing 104 website: https://makercomp.wordpress.com/

Whitney, A., McCracken, C., & Washell, D. (2019). *Teaching Writers to Reflect: Strategies for a More Thoughtful Writing Workshop*. Portsmouth, NH: Heinemann.

Wilde, O. (1890). *The Picture of Dorian Gray*. Oxford University Press.

Winterson, J. (1993). *Written on the Body*. Knopf Canada.

Winterson, J. (1997). *Oranges Are Not the Only Fruit*. New York: Grove Press.

Yancey, K. (1998). *Reflection In The Writing Classroom* (1 edition). Logan, Utah: Utah State University Press.

YouthTruth. (2017). YouthTruth | Learning from Student Voice: College & Career Readiness 2017. Retrieved August 26, 2018, from YouthTruth website: http://youthtruthsurvey .org/college-career-readiness-2017/

Index

About the Authors

Dr. Troy Hicks is a professor of English and education at Central Michigan University and focuses his work on the teaching of writing, the intersections of literacy and technology, and, more broadly, teacher education and professional development. A former middle school teacher, he collaborates with K–12 colleagues and explores how they implement new literacies in their classrooms. Hicks directs CMU's Chippewa River Writing Project, a site of the National Writing Project, as well as CMU's and the Master of Arts in Learning, Design & Technology program. An ISTE Certified Educator, he frequently conducts professional development workshops related to writing and technology.

Also, Hicks is author of the Heinemann titles Crafting Digital Writing (2013) and The Digital Writing Workshop (2009) as well as a co-author of Because Digital Writing Matters (Jossey-Bass, 2010), Create, Compose, Connect! (Routledge/Eye on Education, 2014), Connected Reading (NCTE, 2015), Research Writing Rewired (Corwin Literacy, 2015), Coaching Teacher-Writers (Teachers College Press, 2016), Argument in the Real World (Heinemann, 2017), and From Texting to Teaching (Routledge/Eye on Education, 2017). His edited collection, Assessing Students' Digital Writing (Teachers College Press, 2015) features the work of seven National Writing Project teachers. Hicks has authored or co-authored over 30 journal articles and book chapters and blogs regularly at hickstro.org.

In 2011, he was honored with CMU's Provost's Award for junior faculty who demonstrate outstanding achievement in research and creative activity, in 2014 he received the Conference on English Education's Richard A. Meade Award for scholarship in English Education, and, in 2018, he received the Michigan Reading Association's Teacher Educator Award.

He can be followed on Twitter: @hickstro

Andy Schoenborn is a high school English teacher and award-winning author at Mt. Pleasant Public Schools in Michigan. He focuses his work on facilitating promising writing practices, encouraging teacher-writers, and professional development. As an advocate for teaching, he welcomes pre-service students into his classroom where they can learn and grow in collaboration. Schoenborn is a past-president of the Michigan Council of Teachers of English, Region Representative for the Michigan Reading Association, teacher consultant for CMU's Chippewa River Writing Project, an affiliate of the National Writing Project, co-facilitator of the #TeachWrite Twitter chat for teacher-writers, and he frequently conducts professional development workshops related to writing and pedagogy.

Schoenborn is also a contributing author of Using Technology to Enhance Writing (Solution Tree, 2014), Continuing the Journey 2 (NCTE, 2018) and co-author of Creating Confident Writers for High School, College, and Life (W. W. Norton, 2020). In November 2019, Schoenborn was honored with the 2019 Linda Rief Voices from the Middle Award for outstanding publication for his article, "Reclaiming the Arts in English Language Arts." He is available for hands-on seminars, workshops, and presentations.

In 2013, he was honored with MCTE's Ray Lawson Excellence in Teaching Award "For faithful service, inspirational qualities, and distinguished leadership, in 2014 he received the Great Lakes Bay Region RUBY Award "Recognizing the Upward, Bright, and Young," and 2017 he received the Saginaw Chippewa Indian Tribe's ISE Award "Inspiration, Support, and Encouragement."

He can be followed on Twitter @aschoenborn.